Gold Miner's Daughter

A Memoir of Boom, Bust and
Bliss in the High Sierra

Gold Miner's Daughter

*A Memoir of Boom, Bust and
Bliss in the High Sierra*

Mabel W. Thomas

edited by Laura R. Thomas

ISBN #: 978-0-692-81808-4

Cover design by Rio Vista Graphics, Oakland, CA
Book design by Margaret Copeland/Terragrafix.com

Gold Miner's Daughter is available by special order at your local
bookstore; also online at www.indiebound.org.

Contact Laura Thomas at ciaolauretta@comcast.net.

Contents

For my brother, my cousins, our children and theirs,
a gift of remembering bestowed long ago

Preface

My great aunt, Mabel Winifred Thomas, was old and shapeless when I was a child. She wore her white hair coiled in the back of her head into a little twist, similar to how she appeared in her 1897 graduation picture from San Jose Teacher's College. She wore the shapeless print dresses and thick-soled shoes of elderly women then and walked with difficulty.

At family gatherings, she occupied the most comfortable chair, and regarded me with kindly interest. She had been a librarian for 40 years in Oakland and she nurtured my intellect with books.

I received them at every birthday and at Christmas. They were all classics, the best editions: *The Arabian Nights* with illustrations by Maxfield Parrish; a double edition of *Tom Sawyer* and *Huckleberry Finn*, illustrated by Norman Rockwell; *Heidi*; *The Secret Garden*; *Grimms' Fairy Tales* and *Andersen's Fairy Tales* (which I hated) and *Alice in Wonderland* (which I loved the best). When I told her, around age 9, that I wanted to receive a Nancy Drew mystery, she replied gently, "Well… I don't know whether I approve of that." I realized she thought it was common literature, and yet she gave it to me, bowing to my wishes.

Aunt Mabel sat and quietly recounted her stories, of her family and her life growing up in Grass Valley and Sierra City, and now, 50 years later, I cannot specifically remember a single one as she told it. Instead I have had this manuscript, which she worked on with my grandfather's assistance for over a decade, along with a tract on family history, a couple of chapters about her childhood, family letters, and documents from her career. I have also reminisced with my cousins about our years growing up surrounded by old relatives born in the 1800s who remembered riding the stage and surviving San Francisco's "great fire." Now, we wished we had listened better.

I do remember feeling that she wanted to transmit a legacy, a set of values to us: That we weren't to forget her parents' arrival in the northern Mother Lode from Cornwall, on the southwest coast of England, and Pennsylvania.

More than 75 years later, she could see societal changes that I know she found disheartening and sought solace in recalling her childhood with my grandfather in the rugged Sierra Buttes. She wanted us to remember so the experience of a time and a way of life, so tied to her father's roots and to her own identity, wouldn't be lost. It's all terribly sentimental, but in actuality, it's in stories that our sense of the past and who we are in the present is contained and passed along. Before the creation of media idols for public consumption, it's how we once received the myths and legends that inspired us.

In describing her life for the reader, I have been tempted to mythologize or create a more exciting persona for her. I sometimes wish she had been outspoken and defiant in her youth, like the Pankhurst sisters in England or a reckless flapper in a 1920s jazz club, when she was most likely sitting at her desk in the old Oakland Main Library on 14th Street (now the African-American Museum and Library) toiling quietly at her job of helping the citizens of Oakland read and obtain information.

While it's more marketable to tell the story of the non-conformist, the fearless groundbreaker, I realize telling the story of a life free of stereotypical fanfare is much more complex, and fascinating.

But in some ways I don't have to worry about inventing her. Aunt Mabel tells us in her own words. It's a revealing

Mabel Thomas (second from right) spent 40 years at the Oakland Public Library. This photo is probably taken before 1920 in the main library on 14th Street. When the new main library was built in 1950, this Carnegie library building from 1902 was renamed the Charles S. Greene Library and now houses the African-American Museum and Library. *Thomas Family Photo*

and intimate story of being a child with both freedom and duties, observing a world both natural and man-made, one full of love and certainty amidst major unpredictability.

Her voice is that of an adult recalling childhood sensibilities with a tone of schooled, almost aloof, detachment, yet I don't fail to feel her emotions in certain moments.

Aunt Mabel's memories of five years at the Sierra Buttes Mine is part of an era and a way of life long gone; my childhood encompassed the 1950s and 60s, and I, too, have become inspired to look back and reassess it as an adult and appreciate some of its marvels. And so it goes, generation after generation.

And I am drawn to her story because, born in 1878, my great aunt became a modern woman. Like many in her time, no matter how remote their location, being able to read opened up the world and she gained a sense of independence and agency from it. She lived her later life with a quiet sense of determination and mission and wondrous appreciation of the natural and spiritual world. I know she exemplified countless women of her time in California and elsewhere who rose to embrace what opportunities existed for them while retaining values they were not willing to toss away.

She was ever loyal to her mother, her brother and his family, perhaps partly due to the tragic death of their younger brother at the age of 20; she was surrounded by women at the library that she supervised and encouraged; she never married, but had a couple of close women friends with whom she lived in middle age. She didn't seem to seek recognition for herself. She never rose to be Head Librarian though she substituted for and advised the well-known

In working with her assistants, Mabel Thomas (right) acted as a mentor as well as supervisor. She served as Chief Reference Librarian and Assistant Librarian but was never considered for the job of Oakland's City Librarian, a post held by men until the 1950s. *Thomas Family Photo*

Charles S. Greene (former editor of Overland Monthly) who ran the library from 1899 to 1926.

She published a bibliography of California local history and was the guide and sponsor for a history of Oakland done by the Works Progress Administration in 1938. She stood in the shadows, reluctant to place herself in any kind of footlight. Aunt Mabel's reticence just makes me determined to put her out there, for secretly, she may have wanted it.

Like many women of her time and especially those of religious convictions, she did her work almost under-cover, with motives perhaps unknown even to herself. But ultimately, she did want her own tale told and she began to write it. This memoir only covers five years of her childhood but it's rich in reflection, both on the beauty of her surroundings and the resilience of the boom-and-bust society she lived in and on her own perception of herself, on the woman she was to become.

It's part of a legacy 19th century Californians left to all of us: a sense of identity based on the excitement of experiencing a frontier society evolving into its unique corner of American culture. For the generations that have followed it's what has helped us feel rooted in this marvelous place.

— Laura Thomas
Alameda, California
2016

Foreword

Mabel Thomas' story really begins with her father, Stephen, who was 17 when he left Cornwall, England, as part of a diaspora that started as a trickle in the early 19th century and became an avalanche by the 1870s. The opening of mines in the New World led to Cornishmen settling in Australia, South Africa, Canada and the U.S. Even Stephen's father, William, left for a time to be an overseer in a mine in Cuba in the 1830s.

Stephen Thomas, Mabel's father.
Thomas Family Photo

The reputation of the Cornish of that generation was one of courageous virility and endurance. "They were of the fighting, hard-drinking school. Magnificent men many of them — tall, muscular, upright," English historian A.K. Hamilton Jenkin wrote about those who first went abroad.[1]

William and Elizabeth Thomas, Stephen's parents,
remained in Cornwall while most of their children
emigrated to the U.S. *Thomas Family Photo*

In a photo with his wife, Elizabeth, William appears
tall and proud, with a hand on his wife's shoulder. They are
probably still young. It's years before they would send off a
daughter and all three of their sons to seek better lives in
America and new roots with other Cornish emigrants in
Northern California.

Cornwall, on the southwestern coast of England, had
been a traditional tin mining region since 1000 B.C. Tin is a

great alloy metal and is found in alluvial deposits as casserite and is black or purple in color. Casserite is also found in quartz and may perhaps be why the Cornish were so adept at prospecting gold-bearing quartz lodes in the New World.

Copper too was mined in Cornwall and was at its peak when Stephen was born in 1849 in Porthtowan, at the heart of what is designated today as the Cornwall and West Devon Mining Landscape[2], one of the richest in the world then. Despite the noisy and bleak atmosphere, with the mines' tall pumping engines splayed across the countryside, Stephen remembered the beauty of the cliffs and the Atlantic Ocean.

He began mining along with his father at 8 years old. He often loaned his mother money and when she paid him back, she would say, "but son, I must have it again." Their struggle and the careless manner in which his father spent his earnings at the public house made an impression on

Porthtowan, on Cornwall's northern coast, where Stephen Thomas was born in 1849. *Undated postcard*

him. Mabel wrote that he resolved not to drink or smoke and "developed the Spartan resolution which he perceived to be lacking in his father."

Stephen was also fiercely attracted to music, taught himself to play the flute and coronet and read music and was very devoted to the Methodist Church. He brought a Bible and a copy of *Pilgrim's Progress* with him to the U.S. He also never respected the notion of social rank and angered his parents by not tipping his hat to the local parson.

Despite the prosperity of the copper mines, her father saw little opportunity for himself there outside of constant hard work, Mabel noted in the family history she prepared before launching her memoir: "His cousin Cyrus Penrose had been home on a visit from the United States with what seemed a fortune," she recounts.

Stephen's older brother, also named William, left for the U.S. and sent for Stephen a few years later. Stephen's first stop was in the anthracite mining region of northeastern Pennsylvania in 1866 where he found the hours shorter and the work easier than in Cornwall. He encountered his first labor strike after two days and moved on to another town. He seems to have had, along with that Spartan resolve Mabel noted, a bit of that mythical rugged individualism Americans believe in so completely, as well as a determination to find wealth in the New World that he never gave up until his death.

The mines in Pennsylvania may have reminded him too much of the drudgery he left behind in Cornwall or he was struck by a spirit of adventure for he eventually left for Colorado where he spent a number of years, with a partner, in a mining camp above the timber line.

He missed his first fortune when his partner persuaded him to quit a shaft they were sinking sooner than he wanted. It yielded a rich vein to the next prospector. He nearly starved one winter when food supplies were blocked by snow and he and his partner had to dig their way out, surviving on a little bit of cheese.

By 1873, he was in Virginia City and working in the Comstock Lode for Jim Fair, a man who had come to California in 1849, whose good fortune Stephen wanted to emulate. Fair, along with James Mackey, James Flood and William O'Brien, had been buying stock in mines that were depressed all over the lode and making them profitable. He was about to hit the big bonanza that would make him and his partners among the wealthiest men in the world.

Fair planned to hide the wealth of the lode they had discovered until he secured controlling shares in it. According to Mabel, he laid off Stephen and all the other Cornish miners just before the mine's treasure was revealed. "Those damned Cornishmen know too much" is what Fair said at the time, and Stephen told his children years later he should have jumped on that stock as well.

Another chance at wealth missed, he returned to Pennsylvania to join his younger brother John, but went to work in a drug store in Ashley instead of the coal mines and met the niece of one of the owners, Miss Sarah Joslin.

Stephen Thomas did not possess a fortune after nine years of adventure and hard work but he had a certain amount of pocket change. Family legend has it that he had $10,000 saved up. He took a trip back to Cornwall before his marriage and obtained an amethyst ring for his bride. In June of 1875, Sarah, nicknamed "Sadie," and Stephen Thomas visited New York City, staying at the Astor House for a few days before boarding a train and heading to California.

Sarah Joslin Thomas' ancestors were New England puritans who had arrived in Massachusetts in the 17th century. Her family was prosperous, religious, and firmly established in the small Wilkes Barre suburb of Ashley. Yet they must have seen much in Stephen's vigor and determination. His stories of his adventures must have had a certain appeal as all tales of those who had traveled "out west" had for staid Easterners in those times.

Abijah Joslin, Sarah's father, wrote to Stephen that August asking him to report on what opportunities there were for a grocery business.

> "How is the grocery business and how is the meat market? . . . I do not make these inquiries because I have the California fever. No my pulse beats steady; only this — If you and Sadie stay in California and are determined to make it your future home, I sometimes think it will have to be mine too . . . mother seemingly cannot be reconciled to a separation from Sadie."

The couple settled in Grass Valley, which was rapidly becoming a Cornish town. Stephen went to work in the Idaho Mine. The family found a home on Lloyd Street, one of the many that rise up the hill above old Main Street, and there in 1878 Mabel, and later her brother, Willard, were born.

Willard was my grandfather. After the death of his wife in 1950, Willard and Mabel spent their last years working on this memoir — with many chapters never written. This book with appendix material is the result.

The eleven chapters cover the years 1885 to 1890 when they lived with their parents at the Sierra Buttes Mine, in a house bolted to the mountainside, and down in the town in a newly built house that also housed the mine office. There they experienced a world that always compelled them later, as they became settled in Oakland, to flee regularly for sojourns in the Sierra.

Aunt Mabel began her memoir by telling of her early life in Grass Valley, which had been dubbed the Cornish Capital of America.

Introduction —
The Cornish Capital of America

~~~

In 1875, when my newly married parents arrived to make their home, the "quartz city" of Grass Valley had already become the leading mining town of California. It was first settled in 1849 by immigrants attracted by the good grass for their stock. They had not the slightest notion that the pastures on which their cattle were feeding covered the richest piece of small ground in all California.

In October 1850 a miner named George McKnight chanced to stub his toe against a rock in Gold Hill above Boston Ravine, breaking off a piece of rock whose unusual appearance led him to pick it up. It was a piece of white quartz and it gleamed with the shine of free gold.

Nevada County became one of the most important centers of auriferous vein mining in the state and the world. It thrived on the permanence quartz mining offered in contrast to placer mining (washing or digging of stream bed (alluvial) deposits for minerals). Quartz mining offered long term employment in mines, mills, iron foundries; and the county's population developed an intellectual interest in the subject.

When the first Cornishman arrived in Grass Valley, history does not disclose. That it may have been early is indicated by a statement in the *Grass Valley National* of Nov. 5, 1861, that "our mining is for the most part carried on by Cornishmen."

The "quartz city" has also been called "the Cornish capital of America." The stability of quartz mining in Grass Valley led naturally to the formation there of a permanent Cornish colony. "Fifty years ago," writes (local reporter and historian) Edmond Kinyon in the 1940s, "three-fourths of the five to six thousand residents of Grass Valley were of Cornish birth or descent. At this time, despite dilutions by other racial groups, the proportion of Cornish is still predominant."

The Cornish, long before the Christian era, had supplied the world with tin, but the prosperity of Cornwall's mines later tended to vary with the fluctuation in world markets of the prices of tin and copper. Both were low in the 18th century, causing a period of terrible suffering among the miners, succeeded by another deep depression in the middle of the 19th century. It was, in turn, relieved by the discovery of a new resource of the Cornish people which was to prove of greater export value than their tin and copper — the mining skill of their sons.

"Generation after generation of miners, by far the greater number of Cornish birth or descent, have toiled there, son oftentimes following father," writes Kinyon, in *The Saga of the Idaho-Maryland*.

"I have had numerous high-degreed mining engineers praise the mineralogical acumen of miners of the Cornish migration who probably never turned a page of a treatise on mining subjects. With variations, the comment was 'those old Cornish miners taught me all I know about mining'."

The 19th century saw the tradition of centuries in Cornwall break apart.

"An inheritance of skill and knowledge in mining affairs, gained from countless generations of those who had won their living in the local mines, was at last leaving the soil . . . From Nova Zembla to New Zealand, from Cape Horn to Korea, from Klondike to Cape Town; frozen in the Arctic snows, dried to the bone in tropical deserts, burnt out with fever in equatorial swamps, and broiled thin under equatorial suns — in every country of the Old World and the new — the Cornish miner may be found at work, so far-reaching have been the changes wrought by the depression in local mining in the early '70s.

"Emigration, which reached flood tide in the '70s, began in a trickle in the '20s and '30s, when it was directed to Spanish American countries and to the copper mines of Lake Superior. It was a steady stream in the '50s and '60s after the gold discoveries in California and Australia. Between 1871 and 1881, it was estimated, a third of the mining population left the country.

"Many tin-dressing terms are pure Celtic Cornish and not English at all, but through the agency of Cornishmen have found their way into the mining vocabulary of the world, where they may

3

be heard bandied about in the tongues of distant races, who have never heard of Cornwall."[1]

"It was particularly hard," says a recent historian of Cornwall, "for the conservative Cornishman, so proud of his heritage, so deeply attached to his native country, to tear up his roots and leave his home, but for many there was no alternative, and after the collapse of 1866 there was a continuous stream of emigrants to the newly discovered mining areas of other countries — the United States, South America, South Africa, Australia . . . While the population of England and Wales grew steadily at the rate of 13 percent every 10 years, that of Cornwall fell two percent in the '60s, and a further nine percent in the '70s."[2]

It was in that year, 1866, that my father, Stephen Thomas, a boy of 17, left his home in Cornwall, never to return save for short visits to see his mother. Going first to the coal mines of Pennsylvania, he soon journeyed to become a prospector in the new gold fields of Colorado and Nevada. Not until his marriage in 1875 to my mother Sarah Joslin, whom he had met while working in her father's store in Ashley, Pa., did he join his two brothers, who had already set up permanent homes in Grass Valley while working in the deep Idaho Mine.

One of my earliest memories is of that June morning when I awoke to find that a baby brother had come to our house. I was then just five months over two years old, but I think that I recall a few things prior to this, most of them seemingly detached and inconsequential: a fan made of colored paper to amuse me while on a carriage drive with some ladies; delicious apricots given me at Nevada City on the occasion of some celebration when Father's band was playing; the mud pies I dearly loved to compound, flavoring them with a variety of leaves and flower petals; my little tan dog Nelly and my grief when she ran way to live with a neighbor; also the black and white cat, which remained always faithful to us; my little blue silk parasol; my hands being slapped for pulling the table cloth at meal time and

Mabel's baby brother Willard.
Thomas Family Photo

Sarah Ruth Joslin Thomas and baby Mabel.
Thomas Family Photo

being comforted by my beloved Great Aunt Minnie, a major influence in my young life. She was grieved by my naughtiness but tried, as always, to make me want to be good.

We were early taught to pray, beginning with the words:

> Gentle Jesus, meek and mild,
> Look upon a little child.

Later, the Lord's Prayer was substituted for this introduction, but the ending of our nightly petition was always the same, "Make me a good little girl (or boy), for Jesus' sake!"

I was not the first child of our family. A stillborn daughter preceded me, and my own arrival, in appearance a seeming replica of the first girl baby, had caused my parents to wonder whether they were destined to have only feminine progeny. This deepened their joy over the birth of a son. In other respects, he was an improvement over his sister. He was a normally healthy and happy infant, whereas I was repeatedly told of all the trouble I had given, beginning on the very day of my birth, when I had wailed so shrilly and incessantly that someone "had to walk the floor with me all night long." During teething, I developed a mysterious ailment known as "spasms," the remedy being immersion in a tub of warm water. Later, I periodically tortured my unfortunate parents by attacks of "croup," which obliged them to rise in the middle of the night to "work with me," applying hot and cold compresses and evil-tasting nostrums.

I early learned that it is preferable to be blonde, so often did someone remark on seeing us children together, "what a pity she was not the boy!" or "He should have been the girl!" This I seemed to have accepted as I did other phenomena of

Mabel Thomas was born January 1878 in Grass Valley in a house that still stands on Lloyd Street. She was born with a head of striking black hair as shown in this picture of her at six months. *Thomas Family Photo*

nature, without resentment or envy. After all, did they not love me just the same at home?

Perhaps I owed much of this inward security to the presence in our house of a very unusual personage, my beloved Great Aunt Minnie, who came to California as an organizer for the Women's Christian Temperance Union and was present when I was born. As long as she lived, I was quite sure that I loved her equally with my dearest mother. I know now that my grandmother's sister, Minerva "Minnie" Wells, if she were living today, would be a social worker or a deaconess, or if she had lived several centuries earlier, she would have become a nun — perhaps a saint. She called herself a "city missionary." It was her work to visit the poor, sick, and unhappy, to bring spiritual as well as material aid. She had published a book on the Christian life of separation from the "world-holiness," she called it, and that was the life she lived. She actually seemed to live in an atmosphere not altogether of this world.

As soon as I could walk, I would accompany Aunt Minerva on her visits. I remember only two of the houses we visited, and they were very different. One belonged to a colored woman, Mrs. Thompson, who until her death many years later was a devoted friend of my mother, in gratitude, she said, for the help Aunt Minerva brought her at a time when her state was so desperate that she meditated suicide. The second was the beautiful home of Mrs. Edward Coleman, wife of the wealthy owner of the Idaho Mine who was very interested in some of Aunt Minnie's charities.

Among my memories is my first book, which came at Christmas. It was the *Visit of St. Nicholas*, by Clement Moore, with color pictures of the saint and his reindeer. This my mother read to me until I knew it by heart. Another book I recall was "Universal History," in whose illustration I became interested before I was 18 months old. As I turned its pages, I would inquire the names of the various conquerors, Caesars, kings and presidents whose portrait I saw there. To the consternation of my mother and aunt, they found that I could repeat those names, correctly identifying each one. Fearing too great a strain on my small brain, they hurriedly withdrew this and other volumes that they thought might be unduly stimulating.

I was interested in the persons who passed by on Lloyd Street, but I seem to have been oblivious of the magnificent prospect commanded by our house, standing on the summit of the hill between Main and Neal streets, looking eastward to Nevada City and the hills beyond, and with most of Grass Valley spread out beneath us. That house is still there, although altered by the addition of a high basement, a coat of plaster, and a garage, which fills a portion of the garden where pear trees stood.

Their fruit, I recall, was picked green and carefully spread out to ripen in a dark place. I can see only a few features of the house: the guest-room or spare room on the north side of the house where father's band would sit around the table at their weekly practice and where the Christmas stockings would be hung up for Santa to fill; a pantry off the dining room; a covered walk at the rear leading to a well on the south side and a summer kitchen opposite. This wood range would be set up every spring, to be moved back into the house at the approach of winter.

Of the food cooked I remember only the vegetables brought to the door in two baskets balanced by the Chinese vendor on his shoulder, and one single longitudinal slice of mother's "Graham Bread," lavishly buttered and spread with syrup. Made of whole wheat flour and baked in a round pan it was something to dream about.

I remember vividly a feeling of loneliness as I played about close to our fence and communed briefly with another tiny girl who had just moved into the house adjoining us on the south. Alas! The new neighbor Mrs. Douglas was a woman of some eccentricities, one of them being a refusal to allow her daughter to play with other children. So little Winnie never came again to speak with me through the garden wall.

I watched passers-by on our street, especially the large family of Samuels children, whom I saw on Sundays setting out on a walk with their merchant father. Later, we too would walk with our father in the woods not far distant. On week days I seldom failed to see our cousins' grandfather, Mr. Henwood, on his way home from the mine. In the dinner-pail swinging from his hand, I knew there would be a bit of pound cake saved for me. Sometimes a neighbor's daughter, Lizzie Robinson, would come to help Mother care for us children, and on a certain day of the week Mrs. Dunn would appear to do our family washing. I was fascinated by the pipe she smoked and her habit of seeming to fall asleep as she rhythmically rubbed the clothes up and down on the washboard.

Danger, frightful danger, came one day in the person of a boy who showed me his pocket knife with the avowed intention of cutting off both my ears. One day this miscreant chanced to meet me as I walked down Neal Street hill with Father. My screams when I saw the boy told my father all he needed to know and he made after him as he tried to escape by running down the hill. Retribution came when the boy stumbled and fell, my father on top of him, and the fear that overtook him must have dispelled all further desire to amuse himself by tormenting me.

About three blocks around the corner and up Neal Street lived Uncle John, Aunt Annie, and our three cousins, Willie, Johnny and Freddy. When the two oldest came over to play with us, my sup of woe began to fill. It ran over the day they kidnapped and buried my doll.

It is strange how little I realize what the coming of our grandparents meant in that last year of our life on Lloyd Street. They had visited Aunt Minerva in Oakland, and had consulted a famous surgeon in San Francisco regarding grandfather's illness. His condition was indeed serious but they journeyed to Grass Valley to be with us.

Mother often told us of those last days with the father who was so dear to her, of his patience in suffering and his firm faith in a future life. He drew comfort from a vivid dream in which he talked with a sister who had died. (This dream seems rather remarkable because it was contrary to the conceptions of "the other world" common then and even today.) As she talked, his sister sewed busily upon some garment. This surprised him, as did the absence from this dream of his mother. "Mother went higher long ago," said his sister, who went on to explain that life beyond death has many states and is progressive, and that she herself found much to do in helping others.

The dear man died in Grass Valley on June 9, 1882. His grave is in the Masonic Cemetery there. When grandmother left us to return to the old home in Ashley, Aunt

Minerva Wells went with her. Neither was ever to return to California. Mother was not without hope of soon returning to Ashley, for our father had promised not to remain in the Idaho Mine should another serious accident occur there.

My last memory of the Lloyd Street home is of standing with Mother at the window watching for him when he was unexpectedly late. Although she was slow in hearing it, already news of an Idaho disaster was spreading through Grass Valley. When Father at last appeared, Mother greeted him in disappointed tones: "I expected you to be bringing your digging clothes with you." "Oh," he replied, "I shall not need them anymore. We are leaving Grass Valley."

❦

Editor's note: Mabel traveled with her family to Ashley, Pennsylvania, to stay with their Joslin and Wells relatives for two years. The family came back to Grass Valley, however, when Stephen was hired by the Sierra Buttes Mine as leader of the company's band. Initially going up the high mountain on his own, he could no longer endure the hardships of single life and asked the family to join him.

From Grass Valley, there were just two directions in which to travel; one either "went below" or "went above." By far the more popular choice was to "go below," by way of the little narrow gauge railroad to Colfax, to board an overland train westbound to "the city" (San Francisco) or eastbound to points outside the state.

Destined to "go above," Mabel, her mother and brother Willard had no choice save to proceed by stagecoach from

Nevada City, their only means of reaching the high mountain glimpsed from their Grass Valley hilltops.

The Downieville stage standing in front of the St. Charles Hotel in Downieville. *Courtesy of the California History Room, California State Library, Sacramento, California*

CHAPTER 1

We Go Above

It was still dark at five o'clock on that October morning in 1885 as we three travelers, dressed for the journey, stood awaiting the stagecoach for our trip "above."

On the day before, we had said goodbye to relatives and friends in Grass Valley, and Mother, with such small help as could be rendered by me at age 7 and little brother, had finished the packing of our household furniture for transport by freight team. We had spent the night in the quietest hotel in Nevada City, a temperance house.[1]

We were ready none too soon, for the stage did not keep us waiting.[2] A photograph made in 1893 shows the Downieville stage much as I remember it on that morning, with its great iron-bound wheels, its shabby leather curtain, its racks on top and at the rear for bags and trunks, and its high front seat, on which perched the driver and one or two favored passengers.

Hitched to this vehicle were four horses of a most dejected aspect, as though anticipating the toilsome journey before them. The horses, as we were soon to learn, would be changed every 10 to 15 miles, but unhappy passengers who, like ourselves, were going all the way from Nevada City to Sierra City, could look for no such speedy relief.

The Downieville stage in its daily progress had to cross all three main forks of the Yuba River, together with uncounted minor tributaries, as it wound its way along the recent toll roads that followed old trails worn by 49ers up and down river gorges and across mountain ridges. These trails had followed paths used by Indian hunters in pursuit of wild animals, which had first made them ages before on their ways to and from the water courses.

With some difficulty and aided by the driver, we managed to climb up the steep side into the coach. It disturbed Mother to find a rear seat occupied by a Wells Fargo messenger, his shotgun guarding an express box. However, he proved to be a kind and helpful companion, arranging a bed of mail sacks on the floor of the coach on which we could settle poor little Brother, who suffered all through the long day from motion sickness. Mother and I wore "dusters" of gray or beige linen, and Mother had tied a veil over her hat as additional protection from the thick clouds of dust through, or rather in, which we should travel.

Crossing Deer Creek bridge and leaving Nevada City, our course first led down the steep 10-mile "Purdon Grade" to "Purdon's Crossing" of the South Fork of the Yuba River. This bridge had earlier been known as Webber's, but originally as Wall's.[3] Our next point of interest proved to be North San Juan, which, other than its name, seemed to have nothing of the Spanish. We might rather have fancied ourselves in a New England village as we entered a street lined with white houses set well back in gardens and orchards.[4]

The stage drew up before a hotel since destroyed by fire. I remember the dining room with French windows opening on the street where we sat down to our belated breakfast. We were offered a choice of ham and eggs, bacon and eggs, or steak and eggs, served with cooked cereals, potatoes and hot cakes. We learned that it was the unvarying morning menu in every mountain inn. We saw a number of buildings built of brick so commonly used in the Northern mines. All seemed prosperous, but we were looking at a dying town.

North San Juan had begun as a placer mining center in 1859 and for years served as a principal supply town for the great hydraulic gold mines that had developed along the San Juan Ridge, site of the Malakoff Diggings and many others. Here the world's first long-distance telephone line had been set up to operate the vast system of flumes and ditches bringing water for these mines down from higher in the Sierra.

Not two years before this day of our journey, Judge Alonzo Sawyer had pronounced his famous injunction, which spelled the end of California's hydraulic mining industry, paralyzing all this activity and leaving an estimated $400 million unmined along the ridge.[5]

At San Juan, we were 600 feet below Nevada City and still another plunge downward was before us on the way to the famous Freeman's Crossing of the middle fork of the Yuba. Two deep canyons came together at this spot, as Oregon Creek with its covered bridge joined the Middle Yuba less than a half mile above the crossing. And here we heard the story of the great flood two years before, which had destroyed a covered bridge at the crossing.[6]

It was caused by the breaking on June 18, 1883, of the English Dam, situated on the headwaters of the Middle Yuba about six miles above the present Milton Dam.[7] A 100-foot wall of water rushed down the canyon, sweeping away everything in its path. The Oregon Creek bridge was lifted from its piers and deposited 150 feet below its original place. The Downieville stage to Nevada City had just crossed the Freeman Bridge and moved 100 yards beyond it when the bridge was struck and carried away. Several feet of water ran through Freeman's two-story hotel, while his blacksmith and carpenter shops disappeared.

It is thought that the flood hastened the end of the long dispute between the valley farmers and hydraulic miners. Officers of the Milton Mining and Water Co., which owned the dam, entertained a strong suspicion that it had been blown up by powder, which contributed to the resentment felt in the mining counties against their valley neighbors.

As we crossed the middle fork of the Yuba, we entered Yuba County, and the road began to mount the slopes above Oregon Creek on the way to Camptonville 1,000 feet above the creek. It was a sufficiently tedious climb, for the old road makers had given little thought to easy grading or nice adjustment of curves, and our poor horses made but slow progress in pulling the heavy stage up the hills. The heat of the day and the depth of dust in the roads added to our discomfort, not to mention the rocks over which the stage jolted, dislodging passengers from their seats.

In a spot where trees hung over the road, Mother chanced to observe suspended from a limb one of her dining room chairs, and was not greatly cheered as perhaps she should have been by this evidence of good speed made by our furniture freight.

The present-day motorist driving from Nevada City to Sierra City may catch on one side or the other an occasional glimpse of what looks like a piece of an old dirt road. It is our ancient stage road, which practically paralleled Highway 49 as far as Camptonville, after which the modern driver will not again see its traces until after leaving Downieville. The highway bypasses Camptonville and begins a descent into the beautiful canyon of the North Yuba River through which it makes the rest of the way up to Sierra City.[8]

But our party is still in the old stagecoach with its four horses straining to pull the heavy load up the Camptonville grade, and horseless carriages and hard-surfaced roads are still in the unknown future. Camptonville at last! We were happy to learn that this town was the halfway point on our journey. Here, when winter snows were deep, the up bound stage and its passengers would tarry for the night before changing to a sleigh and putting the horses on snowshoes for a second day of travel.

Before the construction in 1859 of the Henness Pass Road, Camptonville had been an important trading center, the terminus of the freight road from Marysville and the transfer point from which all supplies going up the north fork of the Yuba River to Goodyears Bar, Downieville, Sierra City, and scores of other camps, must be packed in on mule back. Camptonville is said to have been moved twice to make way for hydraulic diggings, and vast scars show the extent of the operations there.[9]

Leaving Camptonville, we found ourselves on the old Yore toll road to Downieville, which first turned eastward and then made its way up and along famous Gold Ridge, passing between the deep canyons of Oregon Creek to the south and the North Yuba to the north. Three miles from Camptonville stood Sleighville House, a two-story hotel. Peter Yore had built it in 1849. Nearby lay the Yore family burial ground, in which one of the inscriptions dates to 1853.[10] We were now in Sierra County and on one of the main freight roads from Marysville to the Comstock. Anxiously our driver listened for the bells on the freighters' mules, for only in certain spots on the narrow road would it be possible for two vehicles to pass.

As we gained altitude, the character of the forest changed. The yellow pine trees were taller and "Digger" pines, madrones, and live oaks were replaced by firs, incense cedars, and black oaks. The road climbed nearly to the summit as it continued northeasterly across the ridge. A diarist, Madame Giovanni, who journeyed from Marysville to Downieville in 1852 left a description of our route, for the ridge was one of her "plateaus."[11]

> "Our trail forced us constantly to ascend mountains almost to their summits, and while descending this panoramic view disappeared from sight; but at the summit of each mountain scaled there stretched a plateau from which the eye could see in every direction an endless chain of ranges that unfolded like the waves of a swelling sea, all covered with dense forests of oak and pine that measured, almost without exception, from one to two hundred feet in height.

"Since the creation of the world to which the giants of nature seemed to belong, the thickness of their foliage had, I believe, prevented a single ray of light from penetrating to the ground. I have never seen anything to compare with the quiet calm of this dense forest . . . The vegetation was luxuriant; under this lush growth the hand of nature had spread a carpet of green moss, thick, soft, and so deep that neither sun nor snow could penetrate to its depths . . . I was profoundly and deeply impressed at the sight of growth so rich, so fertile, so fresh, and at the same time so primitive."

What a change had 30 years brought about in the magnificent forest as seen by Madame Giovanni. It was now comprised largely of smaller trees of a younger growth. Only occasionally did we come upon a giant Sugar or Ponderosa Pine that had escaped the lumberman's axe and the ravaging forest fires. Gone was the carpet of moss, and the sun now shone upon an under growth of shrubbery, flowers, and grasses.

The driver now congratulated us on having completed the most difficult part of the journey when we reached the top of the Gold Ridge ascent. We could now look forward to an easy descent of the Mountain House grade, which he said was the most dreaded part of his return journey the next day.

Except for the Wells Fargo messenger, we were now the only passengers, and Mother listened with interest tinged with some alarm to an exchange of anecdotes between him and the driver, in which stage robberies figured.

One story involved a man named Gregor who the driver said worked a mine in one of those canyons down across the creek from Forest City, not far from Hell's Half-Acre.

"Saving your presence Ma'am," turning to my mother, he said "that is what they called the place. Every now and then, on a Saturday, Gregor would take his wife and drive in his buggy over to Forest, and if there was to be a preaching in the Methodist Church there, they would stay overnight and attend the service. It happened one Saturday that he had made a late start and was hurrying along, not caring to be out on the road after dark. His wife was by his side, and at her feet was the sack of bullion from his mine clean-up that he was taking to the Forest express office.

As they were rounding a sharp turn at a pretty swift clip, suddenly there was a tall man standing by the road side. His left hand was raised, and he was shouting, 'Hold up!' and that lady didn't waste any time listening for what the fellow would say next. No, siree! Quicker'n you could say 'Jack Robinson' she had grabbed that sack of bullion and heaved it clear over the side of the road and hurtling down the hill into a clump of bushes. And then she heard him finishing what he had to say, 'The bridge over the creek is out up the Forest road! I thought I ought to warn ye'."

Advertised along the way by signs affixed to trees was Nigger Tent, a stopping place for teamsters, "only house on the road where no Chinese cook is employed." Although the anti-Chinese agitation was then at its height in the mountains, it seemed but a doubtful recommendation for the Nigger Tent cuisine, for the excellence of the Oriental cooks had assured them a permanent place in most hotel kitchens. Nor did our stage stop there for the midday dinner,

but proceeded onto the rival hostelry, the Mountain House.
Both dated back to the early years of the Gold Rush.

Nigger Tent (first kept by a Negro) was a way station on
the pack trail to Downieville in 1849.[12] A tavern was erected
on the site of the original tent and was dignified with the
name "Sierra Nevada House." The old appellation persisted,
however, into the '80s and '90s, when it was kept by the
Romargi family.[13] Their reputation was more than doubtful,
and in the '80s there were legends of disappearing travelers,
robber bands, and violent deaths.

It was certain that shootings had occurred there that
had never been investigated, and a series of highway robberies had been traced to the grandson, Algie Romargi.
After his death in Folsom Prison in 1882, Mrs. Romargi, a
woman of resolute spirit, clung to her roadhouse almost to
her death in 1899.

An inn known as the Mountain House was a stopping
place as early as 1850[14] "when 2,500 mules carried supplies in pack trains over narrow and precipitous trails to
Downieville."[15] It was now not only the stage house but
the residence of Daniel T. Cole, a principal owner of the
stage line and known because of his lively interest in state
politics as the "emperor of Sierra County." His house had
in the '60s been noted for its annual balls, and his birthday was still celebrated there in royal fashion. Adding to the
charm of the place were the "emperor's" two lovely grand-
daughters, who were being educated at schools "below"
but who might be seen riding their horses over the trails
during summer months.

At the Mountain House, our road forked, one branch
leading easterly and southward to Forest City, Alleghany,

Mountain House Inn, opened in 1850 and shown here in an undated photo, was the last stop Mabel, her mother and brother made before making their treacherous descent into Goodyear's Bar.

and the old Henness Pass road to Comstock. Our way to Downieville went due north and down the headlong descent known as the "Mountain House Grade," surely never to be forgotten by any traveler who has once experienced it.

Again from *The Journal of Madame Giovanni*:[16]

"The trail permitted only one person or one mule to pass at a time. In certain places it was so terrifying as to produce vertigo, for, being scarcely 18 inches wide, if the mule's foot slipped the traveler would undoubtedly roll with it to the bottom of the Yuba, that is, into an abyss two or three thousand feet deep . . . Few caravans reached

Downieville without having to deplore the loss of some mule that had fallen with its load . . . I must confess I was seized with dizziness and fright when I saw what passes had to be crossed."

The stage road which replaced Madame's mule-trail was itself none too wide, and it was so steep that we were alarmed to find the driver taking it at what seemed to us a highly dangerous speed, in contrast to the slow progress which marked our upward climb. Perhaps halfway down the grade, we came to an abrupt stop.

The driver's sharp ear had detected the sound of bells from an up-bound freight team on this narrow, winding road, where it would be so difficult to pass. Having selected the most favorable spot available, he maneuvered his coach and horses into a position as close as possible to the upper bank, and there we awaited, with such calmness as we could summon, the slow approach of the team.

The ensuing altercation between the two drivers, each refusing to undertake the perilous outer passage, might have been amusing had we not been so greatly concerned. A rule of the road required the down-coming vehicle to take the outside, but our driver stubbornly refused to move from his vantage point, invoking the higher rule of "women and children first," and the other ended by accepting the risk. We admired the skill with which he manipulated his 10-mule team with his two lumbering wagons past us and up the grade in safety.

Without further incident we resumed and finished our headlong descent into Goodyears Bar, and were by this time so benumbed by the day's fatigues that we almost failed to be interested in our first passage over the North Yuba, by way of the old Yore's Bridge, and our entry into Downieville.

Here the old toll road came to an end, and the Sierra Turnpike, which in 1870 had replaced the old mule-trail into Sierra City, took us, with a new driver, on the final stage of our journey.[17] This narrower and rougher road, like its successor, the present Highway 49, led up the magnificent canyon of the North Yuba River beyond Downieville.

Leaving after 4 o'clock, it was not long before darkness came upon us in this deep and narrow gorge. Even so, we saw something of the mining activity along the way. Here, where every foot of the river's bed and banks had been searched by thousands of miners in '49 and '50s, there still remained a little gold to reward the patient gleaning of small companies of Chinese.

Great scars along the hill slopes told of hydraulic washing only so recently discontinued, while some surreptitious hydraulicking was yet being carried on in recesses of the river's tributary canyons. In some of these were flourishing quartz mines, which were now the chief dependence of the county.

On the south, as we proceeded up the river, we passed the beautiful Secret Canyon, the Jim Crow Ravine with its Comet Mine, Nigger Canyon, where the Cleveland Mine was later developed, Charcoal Ravine, Keystone Ravine with its Keystone Mine, the Marguerite Mine near Loganville, and the Avalanche Ravine in the environs of Sierra City. Near Loganville on the north was the extensive Ladies Canyon, and a little beyond was the western spur of Sierra Buttes Mountain, on which an upward glance might have caught a glimpse of the lights of the Buttes Mine boardinghouse.

The October darkness had fallen before the Downieville Stage, in which at five o'clock that morning we had left Nevada City, rolled into Sierra City. Although it was our first experience, we did not fail, as we passed successively through North San Juan, Camptonville, and Downieville, to learn something of our driver's technique.

He was expected to make an impressive entrance into town. No matter how steep and long the grades they had traversed, the horses would take on new life and quicken their pace when reaching the purlieus of any considerable settlement. The stage must speed up enough to enable the driver to pull up with a grand flourish upon reaching the stage stop.

So it was that we received but a blurred impression of Sierra City as we were carried at a gallop up its main street, followed by a queue of shouting boys and barking dogs. A sudden stop before the town's principal inn, Scott's Hotel, brought three exhausted and dust-encrusted passengers to the end of their day's journey, and there stood Father, waiting to welcome us to our new home.

The nearly 9,000-foot-high Sierra Buttes peaks dominate the skyline over Sierra City and entranced Mabel Thomas when she arrived in Sierra City in October 1885. *Courtesy www.nevadarambler.info*

CHAPTER 2

The Old Man Watches the Sky

Could I ever forget my first sight of the Sierra Buttes Mountain as I stood with Brother the next morning in front of Scott's Hotel? We were still in shadow, but the sun was shining on that peak just visible over the roof of the Busch Building across the street, one of Sierra City's finest. But we had eyes only for the giant rock which topped the summit of the mountains.

"Oh, Papa!" I exclaimed as our parents joined us, "I want to go to that big rock. Please take us there before breakfast."

"Quite a climb!" replied my amused father. "Do you think we would be back in time for breakfast?"

"Just how far is it?" Mother inquired.

"Well, it's a 9,000-foot peak. That would make it about a mile if we could fly straight up from here. Walking the trail would make it quite a few miles farther," my father explained. "They don't usually figure on less than a whole day for the trip up and back. Once you are there, you want to stay awhile to take in the magnificent view of mountain ranges and lakes and rivers, and the Sacramento Valley with

The Busch building in Sierra City housed a general store, post office, Wells Fargo Express office and the headquarters of E Clampus Vitus. *Courtesy of the Sierra County Historical Society*

its trains running and the smoke from the engines, and Mt. Diablo and the Coast Range way off in the distance. It's a sight you can never forget."

My "big rock" is not the highest of the many "buttes," but although the northern aspect is quite different, it does from the southern slope appear to dominate all the others, and in Sierra City was always known as "the Buttes rock." It was first climbed by the Indians who were so numerous in this region before the white men arrived.[1]

Downieville miners scaled the mountain in the early '50s naming it "Downieville Buttes" and carved their names on the rocks, which they likened to the teeth of a gigantic saw. Geologists of the State Mining Bureau, coming later, identified the "buttes" in scientific terms, as "a group of volcanic remnants" in the form of "a columnarly jointed lava cap." But we children had our own name, given us by Mother.

"Don't you *see?*" she cried as she studied them that morning, "that rock is a man's head! There he lies looking straight up into the sky, and those small rocks at the side are his arms and legs and feet!" We, who had learned from her to see pictures in changing cloud forms, were now quick to agree.

"You will be nearer the Old Man in our new home up the mountain," promised Father as he led us in to breakfast, "and while we are waiting for the furniture to come, you will be able to do some exploring in Sierra City."

We did walk that day all up and down Main Street, a narrow shelf cut into the foot of the mountain's southern slope in the deepest canyon of the North Yuba River. It was but a little way above that hurrying, swirling stream, which had carved the gorge through which it flows and whose golden bed had lured the first white men to the region. Just across the river, the canyon's opposite wall rises just as steeply but to a lesser height, forming the dividing ridge between the north and middle forks of the Yuba. Oddly enough, the settlement had never crossed the narrow river, but remained confined to the buttes side of the North Yuba.

Main Street was a continuation of the stage road to Downieville on the west and to Sierra Valley over the Yuba Gap on the east. Prior to 1870, there was no road, and no stage-line from the town. All transportation moved by way of trails up or down the steep mountain grades. Those, Father said, were the days of pack mules and oxen, when the legendary driver, Blewberry Jones, became famous along Henness Pass and Yuba Gap as "the champeen cusser of

Syeera County."[2] They were also days of ruinously high freight rates, which lasted until roads were built in 1870.

Except for two "flats" on the lower side near the river, Main Street affords the only nearly level walk in the vicinity. A brief descent not far from our hotel brought us to the larger of the two, "Busch's Flat," a mountain meadow, watered by rivulets on their way to the Yuba, surrounded by trees, and bordered by a number of dwellings, together with the Catholic Church. On this pleasant spot, picnics were held, ball games were played, and here the circus would be set up when it came to town.

"This is where Sierra City began back in 1850," said Father. "The diggings must have been good so close to the river, but it was not a good beginning." He told us the story as he had read it in the new county history.[3]

"Sierra City's real beginning was in 1850 after all, for it was then that the Sierra Buttes quartz-ledge was discovered," he recounted. "The outcroppings were so rich that it almost emptied Downieville when the news arrived there. Everybody rushed up to the Buttes, and the mountain was staked off to the very top. The 'excitement,' as they called it, didn't last very long, and everyone went home again except the miners working on the Buttes and Independence mines."

P.A. Haven and Joseph Zumwalt were about the first white men to arrive in 1850. By 1852, 20 rock-crushing mills known as arrastras, run by mules, were pulverizing rock in the neighborhood, which, with the numerous tunnels piercing the hill in every direction, employed a large working force. Sierra City then consisted of two large buildings (one on the site of the Catholic Church), a baker shop, and several gambling houses and saloons. During the succeeding winter, the town was entirely demolished by the heavy snows and for some years matters did not look very promising for a revival of the settlement.

"We don't build such weak roofs here nowadays," Father said reassuringly, "and now they are made with steep slopes to shed the snow." (We were to remember this story when, only five years later, the Catholic Church at which we were now looking would be destroyed by a similar avalanche.)

"Who was the lucky man who found the mine? Did he become very rich?" asked Mother.

"He was a Mexican named Manuel Gutierrez[4] and a good prospector, for he also discovered the Independence and the Plumas Eureka," Father recounted. "He did well enough at first, but he made the mistake of selling his claims too early. 1850 was also the year of the famous 'Gold Lake excitement.' Hundreds of miners from as far away as Marysville and Nevada City swarmed up into Sierra and Plumas counties hunting for a wonderful lake whose shores were said to be lined with gold nuggets for anyone to pick up."

"Oh! And did they find it?" I cried.

"No, although they climbed all over the country behind the Buttes, where there are scores of lakes, they didn't find the one lined with nuggets," Father said. "They gave the name Gold Lake to one of the biggest lakes in mockery, but the hunt did open up this part of the country, and there was gold here in plenty for those who had the sense to dig for it in likely places. This Buttes district is noted for the number of nuggets which have been found here since then, and the biggest of them all came out of the Monumental Mine, which is part of the Buttes Mine property now. Only one larger nugget has been found in California and only two larger in all the rest of the world.[5]

"One of the men in the party which named our Gold Lake was Philo Haven. He had struck rich diggings in other spots, but he finally took up land around the lake and built a house, where he lives now. He has found some good mines, too, both quartz and gravel, so you see the name they gave the lake is not so funny, after all."

By this time, we were walking back up the hill to Main Street, where we were soon again in front of our hotel.

"Here," Father said. "you can see what has grown out of the old ranch-house where the pack trains used to stop. Scott's Hotel stands where the Yuba Gap Hotel used to stand, built in 1863. August Busch owned it in 1871, when he built the Busch Building across the street."[6]

Busch was, Father thought, the wealthiest man in Sierra City, being one of the principal owners of this new and very rich Young America Mine. He might also be called the Pooh Bah of Sierra City, since his building housed not only his general store, but the post office, where he officiated as postmaster, the Wells Fargo Express office, of which he was agent, and the telegraph office. There was also one of those new telephone lines connecting with the Sierra Buttes Mine on "the hill," where we were going to live. The building's second story was occupied by Mr. Busch's residence, and an outside stairway led up to "Busch's Hall" on the third. Last, but perhaps not least, it served as headquarters for the "ancient order of E Clampus Vitus," which Sierra City knew as the Clampers.

Busch's Flat, as it appeared in 1885, with the No. 9 mill on the left, and the treeless mountainside above. *Thomas Family Photo*

A postcard from the 1920s of old Sierra County miners notes, with droll humor, "all had struck it rich at least once during life." *Courtesy of the California Historical Society*

CHAPTER 3

Boom-town of the Eighties

The town we walked through that October morning in 1885 was nearing the height of its prosperity. When the Reis Brothers sold their Sierra Buttes Quartz Mine to a London company in 1870, Sierra City was a mere small group of buildings at the foot of the trail leading down the mountain from the mine.

It was an isolated hamlet, whose only roads were mountain trails. But from the letter of a Sierra Buttes miner published in the Downieville newspaper, the *Sierra Democrat*, Feb. 28, 1863, it was a lively spot:

> The inhabitants of Sierra City, about a mile below us, at the foot of the mountain . . . with their two hotels and two saloons should probably be able to make the traveling public rejoice. The Yuba Gap route is open and the "express train," (mule train) makes regular trips through. Times have been lively at the "City" this winter. Balls and parties have been the order of the day. Last winter it was impossible to scare up ladies enough to form a set . . . and this dearth has reigned for the

five years I have been a sojourner here . . . The
ladies appear in calico and the gents without their
Sunday clothes . . . When the wagon road is put
through, we hope to be able to mingle more with
the world and show them how well we all look in
our Sunday clothes.

Alas for the writer's optimism! He was to wait seven
years longer for his eagerly anticipated wagon road, when
the new London company, by bearing a large part of the
expense, induced the county supervisors to extend the stage
road from Downieville to Sierra City and thence on to
Sierra Valley over the Yuba Gap.

The new owners of the mine began to build a new boarding house to accommodate a larger work force and with
roads came new mining enterprises, not only on the Buttes,
but up many of the canyons east and west of the growing
town. The old Independence Mine, on the same ledge as the
Buttes, was purchased and revived by the new Sierra Buttes
Mining Co. of London in 1876. Higher up the mountain,
prospectors were opening up the Phoenix, the Buttes Saddle,
and the Mountain mines. The Marguerite Mine began at
Loganville in 1881; the Cleveland, in "Nigger Canyon," two
miles farther down, began work in 1884.

Over the ridge from the Buttes Mine, the Colombo was
employing more than 100 men, and on the north side of the
mountain a new quartz ledge, the Young America, discovered in 1883, was owned by local men and giving promise
of becoming one of the richest mines in all Sierra County.

Now, in 1885, a wagon road already connected Sierra
City with its mill just above Lower Sardine Lake and only

a short distance below Upper Sardine, "that beautiful little cirque lake, nestled under three peaks of the Sierra Buttes, whose appearance tallies so closely with that ascribed by Stoddard to his missing "lake of gold."[1] The Sierra Buttes company was grading a site for its new office below the new No. 9 mill, preparatory to the transfer down to the city of most of its extensive plant at No. 7.

Moved by these signs of growth, Downieville's *Mountain Messenger* had predicted that Sierra City would be the new Virginia City. The *Sierra Tribune* enthusiastically asserted:

> The facts fully warrant us in saying that 'ere another 12 months roll around, Sierra County will have taken the lead above all competitors as the banner mining region in California. In the Sierra City district alone there are at present 90 stamps pounding away night and day on good-paying ore. To our certain knowledge 80 more stamps will be in operation in that vicinity before snow flies next fall . . . The Sierra Buttes Mine will in a few months give employment to between 300 and 400 miners.

The same paper in 1886 named Sierra City as "the best town in the state, north of Nevada City. Twenty to thirty houses could be rented tomorrow at good rates." So strong was this paper's faith in the town's future that it had moved its publishing plant from Forest to Sierra City,[2] which in 1886, had an estimated population of 1,200. The one-room schoolhouse was being enlarged to add a second teacher. Several new houses were under construction, and others already completed were occupied by more than one family.

In June 1884, the *Messenger* had reported the enlargement of Goff's livery stable, a second floor added to Castagna's store, the opening of a second butcher shop, one more saloon, the erection of a Catholic Church to replace one burned in 1882, and such refinements as a soda and ginger-ale factory and a lunch stand serving oysters, while Scott's Hotel, which had been rebuilt in 1873, now had 50 bedrooms and a covered drive and court, which, said the *Messenger*, was like the Palace Hotel in San Francisco.

❦

As we continued our morning walk, the hustle of horse-drawn traffic up and down the street, varied by an occasional mule team with freight, impressed us. There were groups of men lounging in front of every business, most of them tilted back in chairs, others supported against some convenient wall or post. Mother said they made her feel as though she were "running the gauntlet."

"Why are so many men idling here?" she asked. "Isn't there any work for them to do?"

"You shouldn't call these boys idlers," remonstrated Father. "Most of them have been hard at work up in the ravines and gulches, and now their water supply has given out. This is the season when the small streams dry up. I am glad to see so many of them out here in the sunshine instead of drinking or gambling in some saloon!"

A large proportion, Father pointed out, were well past middle age, most of them flotsam and jetsam from the gold rush, lonely wanderers, survivors of many years of incredible hardships.

"I know what such a life has been from my own time spent prospecting in Colorado and Nevada," he said. "Remember what I have told you so often, and now I say it again: Never turn away a man carrying his blankets!"

At this point, our attention was diverted to the sight of a passing rider on a side-saddle, an elderly woman wearing the long-skirted habit and high hat of that day, as though, Mother remarked, attired for a canter in Golden Gate Park.

This dignified lady was Mrs. Orson Bigelow, riding down from her pleasant home higher up on the mountain, which was noted for its garden and orchard. Another surprising sight was a horse, saddled and bridled but minus a rider, approaching at a rapid gait from the upper end of town. "He's on his way home," explained Father, "He's been hired to carry some man to an outlying mine, and these horses have been trained to return to their livery stables on

The J.G. Rose livery stable in Sierra City in early 1900s; in 1885, it belonged to George Abbe. *Courtesy of the Sierra County Historical Society*

being turned loose. No one can catch them on the road and mount them either.[3] He has passed Adam Moore's stable, so he's going to either Goff's or Abbe's."

"Three livery stables in this small place!" Mother exclaimed.

"Oh, they have plenty of business," replied Father. "They have a larger population to serve in the mines outside than here in Sierra City."

"But how many saloons there are!" she observed, "Why, I have counted 10 already."

"They say there are 28 altogether," said Father, "but that counts the four hotels and the two breweries and three dance halls besides two groceries and other places serving liquor."

Listen to this advertisement in the *Tribune*:[4]

Colombo Restaurant, Main Street, Sierra City. Good meals and beds at all hours, fresh oysters always on hand, the best of wines, liquors, and cigars.

Yours truly, J.B. Avignone.

The liquor ads were probably the main support of this paper. Here there is one in rhymes that must have cost something!

When everything looks blasted blue
And misery sticks like Spaulding's glue,
A nip that reaches toe and hair
Will make a man a millionaire.
A scrawny woman looks divine,

My burial lot becomes a mine,
The trees all walk, the fences run,
My funny talk just takes the bun.
Whene'er you want a nip that's nice
As can be bought at any price,
Drop in and see me, don't forget,
I keep the best in town, you bet!
A man's a fool to live in grief
When he can get complete relief
And feel as happy as a clam
By simply calling at Joe Stevens' Bank Exchange!

After reading all the rhymes, Mother was not amused. "I am sorry for the poor men who are attracted by such plain talk about what drinking will do to them. The Good Templars ought to publish an answer to this. But I think I understand better now why a place like Sierra City supports so many saloons."

Spellenberg's saloon. *Courtesy of the Sierra County Historical Society*

We had paused before the old fire bell, which years ago had found rest here after its long voyages around the Horn to San Francisco and a journey to the mines by pack mule over mountain trails.

"Thanks to our plenty of water," Father said, "we haven't had the big fires in Sierra City that have burned out most of the mining towns. If we had, we might have better buildings here now."

Mother was reminded of an article she had read in an *Overland Monthly*[5] magazine that Mrs. Richards had lent her, which told of a trip to Sierra City and up to the top of the Buttes.

"It spoke of 'water from a thousand rills turned loose in this place.' I haven't seen any rills. Where are they?"

"You'll see them next spring," Father said. "Now is the driest time of the year, but a little way up the road there is one they call the Big Spring,[6] which never changes the year round. I'd like to see that article. What else did it say?"

"They drove up to the Buttes Mine," Mother recounted.

"Said the scenery was like Yosemite; then drove on up to Whitney's camp,[7] where they left their carriage to climb the rocks. They picked large lilies up there. I remember their seeing Downieville filled with well-dressed people, 'women in silks, men with goldheaded canes,' but Sierra City was 'only a single street, with a flat near the river and a hotel up a steep little side street,' where rocks had to be used to keep a vehicle from sliding down hill."

"That's Butte Street," laughed Father. "They must have stopped at Mitchell's Hotel. Well . . . Sierra City had done some growing in the two years since those people were here, but it's still the little town at the foot of the big mine. Now I want to show you how the mine is moving down into town."

So we did not turn up Butte Street, which would have brought us shortly into Chinatown and the unsavory neighborhood of the three dance and gambling houses.

Leaving the old fire bell and the Masonic Hall over Mr. Willoughby's clothing store, which stood on the corner, we passed the Goff residence opposite the Goff livery stable, then turned down a driveway which led up past the Kane residence and on to the second of the town's two flats, now, Father told us, to be christened Buttes Park.

This property had become of great importance in 1881, when the Buttes Mine management had planned to drive its No. 9 tunnel under the stage road at a point where it crosses the Reis Ravine.[8] The company had purchased all of the James Kane lands[9] except his house above the flat, and also acquired the Lavezzolo Ranch, which adjoined it on the south. As we reached the Kane home, we found access to the flat blocked by movements of men grading a site for the company's new office, but, looking across the flat to the ravine above, we gained a full view of the new No. 9 mill, the throbbing of whose 60 stamps had been audible since we first entered the town and now that we stood so near seemed to have risen to a continuous roar.

"You become accustomed to it," Father told us, "and would miss it if it stopped. Once, when they closed down the mill late one night, everybody in town woke up! Except for that one short streak, it has been crushing ore day and night since it was completed a year ago last spring."

An aerial tramway had been constructed to roll pay-ore from No. 8 to a large bin level with the entrance to No. 9

tunnel, from which hand-cars conveyed it on a side-track to the new mill. It was fascinating to watch the loaded cars coming down the steep tramway and by their weight pulling the emptied cars back to No. 8, so far above on the mountain.

Turning back to Main Street, we proceeded westward past Soracco's Hotel and the narrow street leading up to the cemetery. We continued past Fischer's Brewery and on

Soracco's Hotel, in wintertime. *Courtesy of the Sierra County Historical Society*

Bigelow House, called Mitchell's Hotel in 1885.
Courtesy of the Sierra County Historical Society

to the bridge over Reis Ravine. Here we were close to the end of the tramway, the rear of the mill, and, most exciting of all, to the new No. 9 tunnel! It now pierced the mountain to a length of 6,200 feet and was still pushing on in its pursuit of the missing vein. In addition, an upraise of 800 feet was under way to the No. 8 level. Already $150,000 had been spent on this work, Father said, without any return to the company, while the new mill had cost an additional sum of $60,000.[10]

"But let us go on," he said. "I want you to see how Main Street is being stretched out along the stage road to Downieville. The owner of this house with the beautiful garden is H.H. Bigelow, brother-in-law to the lady on horseback. He is the man who built Mitchell's Hotel (called Bigelow House at first), and his wife was 'Aunt Jane' to everyone — a good woman! But look at this large lot next door. They are getting ready to put up a mansion here for one of the Young America Mine owners, Watt Hughes. You can see this lot from our new home on the mountain. We should be able to watch it going up."

Other building was proceeding on the opposite (the south) side of the stage road, where in some places it almost hung over the river. Here, opposite the Pianezzi Ranch, Mr. Bigelow was erecting the row of houses for which prospective tenants were impatiently waiting.

We turned to walk back to our hotel, this time passing the town's two butcher shops, Rose's Hotel, Dr. Spedding's office, another brewery, a tin shop, the Good Templars Hall, and a "Boots and Shoes" store. This last one sticks in my memory as the scene of a tragic disappointment.

Having entered it with the intention of purchasing shoes for Brother and me, my parents ignored my preference for a pair of "French kid" shoes with not only the most beautiful pearl buttons but with a crowning glory of tassels. Instead, I was fitted with boy's boots made of cowhide and not even buttoned-laced! I was overwhelmed with grief and cannot recall anything more of our progress back to the hotel where my father left us to return to his work on the mountain, pending the arrival of our furniture.

Mother spent the intervening time to advantage in learning from our landlady, Mrs. Scott, how she performed the seeming miracle of keeping her hostelry free from bed bugs, pests common in mountains inns. Mother had lived for eight years in Grass Valley without encountering them. Father found them to be his second source of agony after his long struggle with the instrumental talent of the miners in his band.

Whether he lodged in the boarding house dormitory or in a miner's cabin, he found himself victim to bed bugs, a nocturnal creature imported from the Old World to torment the new.

Mrs. Scott's victory was not obtained without incessant warfare. On the departure of a guest, the room he had occupied would be stripped of all articles except mattress and wooden furniture. Curtains, carpets, and bedding were cleaned, every crack and crevice on furniture, walls, and ceiling was treated with kerosene. Although Mother was never to relax her vigilance while she remained at No. 7, I can report that our home there was never invaded, and that, after moving down into the town, she gradually ceased to fear it.

It was now possible for Mother to make a more leisurely examination of the city's stores, after which she

Hannah Riley Scott. *Courtesy of the Sierra County Historical Society*

pronounced it "a man's town," in which little consideration was given to feminine needs. The only exception she found in the variety store of Monsieur La Bonté, where she was pleased to see some fine china, ornaments, and even a few books and magazines.

On Saturday evening there was an open meeting of the Good Templars' Lodge, to which we were shepherded by kind Mrs. Scott, Brother and I proudly wearing our badges as members of the Band of Hope, a children's organization

of which there were chapters in Grass Valley and Downieville but, unhappily, none in Sierra City.

To this day I remember hearing a song by Mrs. Kitto, in a voice whose volume would have sufficed to fill a much larger auditorium. Other items of the program are supplied by my good friend at Downieville, the *Mountain Messenger*, which gives the title of Mrs. Kitto's song as "Ask Me Not Who." An essay on temperance was ready by Mr. T. Perryman, who also recited "The Bridal Wine Cup," Mrs. Lewis relieved the solemnity of

Band of Hope Medallion. *Courtesy of Wikimedia Commons.*

the occasion with a comic song, after which Mrs. Freitas "with great pathos" sang "Where Is My Wandering Boy Tonight?" Some excitement was created by the supposed blackballing of a new member, which, on being challenged, turned out to have been an error in counting ballots.

Ah Sin Dai Li was one of the cooks at the Sierra Buttes Mine No. 7 boarding house. He worked for the Thomas family when they later occupied the mine office in town and was given money to return to China by Stephen Thomas. *Thomas Family Photo*

CHAPTER 4

Up the Trail

Sunday morning brought Father in time for breakfast and with thrilling news. Our furniture had arrived and was already installed in the new home on the mountain.

He accompanied us to the little Methodist Church on Butte Street, where we were in time for Sunday school preceding the service, and where Father seated himself in the Bible class of 20 young men, led by one of Superintendent Preston's office assistants.

The sermon was preached by a young Buttes miner, who was also one of the several local preachers among the mine's underground workers. The regular pastor, who resided in Downieville, was on a tri-weekly circuit, serving also the outlying towns of Forest City and Sierra City. He was preaching this morning in the boarding house at No. 7 and would in the evening fill the pulpit here in the Sierra City church.

Reinforced by a final dinner at the hotel, we set out upon the climb up the mountain to No. 7. The mile-long trail would be steep, so old Jesus had come down from the mine with one of his mules, on which to load our handbags. "Old Jesus" was a Mexican, whose black hair and beard surprised us by not looking very old. Up the Buttes Street hill we followed him, past the church, past Mitchell's Hotel, then turning left through the small Chinatown to the foot of the trail. Steep it proved to be, avoiding the perpendicular by a series of zigzags.

"An easy climb when you get used to the altitude," Father encouraged us, regretting that he had not asked Jesus to bring Dolly, his other mule, to serve as a mount for Mother. There were frequent stops to rest, in which Brother and I were glad to join instead of dashing back and forth to explore. Soon we passed the junction of our trail with that to No. 8 and were again within view of the tramway conveying ore from No. 8 down to the No. 9 mill.

Our foot trail occasionally approached an even steeper "timber-chute," and we saw the semicircular ruts which had been worn into its base by the sliding timbers, guided on their passage by Jesus with one of his mules. The timbers, made from large trees higher up the mountain, were for use in shoring up the new tunnels at No. 8 and No. 9. Upper levels of the mine, Father told us, had already consumed a vast forest of timber.[1]

These obscured our view of most of the nearby terrain as we toiled on from one monotonous zigzag to another, and it was with considerable relief that three weary novice climbers finally emerged upon a wagon road by the big barn at No. 7.

"Here we are, home at last!" Father cheered us as we stood looking up and around at this strange new world, built upon a series of narrow shelves cut into the mountain side, one above another, and connected by ascending or interweaving trails. For the next two years, ours was to be the life of mountaineers on the sheer slopes of the Sierra Buttes.

Here the road which had ended our trail forked, one branch turning upward to reach the boarding house and mine offices, the other proceeding on a level to the carpenter and the mill, connecting on the way with another trail leading down to the main entrance into the mine by way of No. 6 and No. 7 tunnels.[2] A short walk along the

These buildings were along the trail to the No. 7 quartz mill. The home occupied by the Thomases was probably off the photo to the left. *Thomas Family Photo*

upward road brought us to a horizontal trail which might be considered the street on which we were to live. Here our attention was fixed on several small cabins, set a considerable distance apart.

"The second one over there is ours," said Father, upon which Brother and I rushed ahead to mount the steps of a narrow veranda extending along the front. (We soon learned that in the architectural vernacular, it was a "stoop.") Impatiently we tried to glimpse the interior by peering through the windows. These and the door appeared at some time long past to have been treated to a coat of paint, the remaining woodwork being left to weather to a dismal gray, which led Mother to form none too rosy an anticipation of what awaited us within.

At last, that door was opened and we were in what was to serve as our combination living-dining room and kitchen. There was a glorious view out of its windows — the Buttes above, with their opposing range of mountains, and river and town deep in the canyon below; but, for the time being, all our eyes were busy with the little house within, in which our familiar furniture had already been disposed by Father.

A bedroom opened off each end of the multi-purpose room, which was fortunately large enough to accommodate the kitchen range, the dining room table, and various other necessary pieces. An ingrain carpet covered most of the floor, the kitchen area being protected by oilcloth.

From our kitchen a rear door led into a lean-to, one end of which served as a woodshed and the other as a summer kitchen. Into this water was piped, a luxury which appeared to have been an afterthought, but it was good to see Mother's face brighten when she saw it. "Stove-moving time" was so nearly come that Father had set up our range in its winter quarters.

Mother was pleased by his arrangement of one of the end rooms as a bed-sitting room with her best Brussels carpet and some of her former parlor furnishings. What she thought of the paper on the walls she did not say, but she had been unable to repress a startled look on entering the front door. The walls had been sealed with tongue-and-groove pine, then covered in places by various issues of the *London Graphic*, among which a Christmas number was conspicuous.

My attention was soon fixed upon what appeared to be a story marching up and down the walls. Having been for a whole week deprived of reading matter (and a week is long when one is 7 years old), I promptly applied myself to its decipherment. It was my first encounter with a ghost story (for which I would later learn that Christmas *Graphics* were famed), and my excitement mounted as the harrowing tale unfolded. Alas! The latter portion had been pasted upside down! I never did learn how it ended, although I was able to read some paragraphs under the window by going outside and suspending myself head down over the story.

Brother in the meantime was far from idle; he explored the outdoors, discovering what seemed to be a small cave just back of the house. It was only a hole abandoned by some miner, Father said, but it excited Brother, who had brought in a quartz specimen showing a gleam that resembled gold.

"No son," Father told him, "Those are only sulphurets, but you will soon learn to know the color of gold up here."

Brother had a question. "Why is this house fastened to the rocks back there?"

"To keep the big winds from blowing us away when winter comes," was Father's reply.

"Is this house in an exposed position then?" asked Mother.

"Oh no, we are really sheltered here, but every building on this hill is either anchored to the rocks by iron rods like this one or shored up by timbers like the boarding house."

As the sun set and the sudden chill of the higher altitude descended upon us, we were glad to gather around the fire quickly kindled by Father in the kitchen range, henceforth to be our only source of added warmth. To hurry the flame he used "pitch pine," rich in resin, which he said we children should learn to gather from old stumps abounding on the mountain side.

Well before 5 the next morning our parents were up, and it took only the sound of the coffee grinder to summon Brother and myself to breakfast, impatient to explore the neighborhood of this new home. With many uncertainties of her own Mother restricted us to our own small yard, enclosed by a fence, at one side of the house.

Here a pile of wood waiting to be sawed and split into stove lengths suggested to my small mind a delightful possibility of a playhouse. Brother, not at first enthusiastic, was coaxed into collaboration, and an area soon marked out at one corner of the fence was outlined by logs dragged from the woodpile. It was heavy work for small arms, and energies had begun to flag when Mother called us to be tidied, ready to go with her on what was to become her regular morning errand to the big boarding house, farther up the hill and reached by a broad trail midway between the two cabins.

On this morning she was especially careful that our faces and hands should be spotless and our garments clean and freshly ironed, although it was only to the company's food store that we were going, and there would be only old John Robinson to see us there in the basement of the boarding house.

"Old John" was himself something of a sight with his gnarled old face and his garb of "blue drilling." For 20 years he had carried the mail to mines on the mountain, which had separate post offices, but now had only the easier work of supplying the boarding house with meat and caring for the company's cattle, driven over from Sierra Valley to a stockade some little distance to the rear of the mine settlement.

He greeted us with something less than cordiality and was firm in restricting Mother's choice of beef to what she considered inferior cuts. The best roasts and tenderest steaks he reserved for the mine's two great personages, Mr. Preston and Mr. James.

To argue the point was hopeless, and Mother was obliged to alter her menu for the day, although she never found herself able to comprehend how two households, together comprising only 11 persons, one of them an infant, could consume all the choicer parts of even one beef animal. From Mrs. James, soon to become an intimate friend, she later learned that the daily allowance of meat for her family included a generous roast, a section of tenderloin sufficient for a number of steaks, and a large round of beef for soup.

We needed a supply of groceries, for which we found we must apply to Thomas Mills, steward of the boarding house, whom we found not only gracious in manner but compliant in service. He had, apparently, an abundance of such staples as flour and potatoes in his stores, but as he explained, he depended for greater variety upon daily deliveries from the town below. Every weekday morning, Tom Dunn, in charge of the mine's stable, would drive his two-horse team over the wagon road to Sierra City, and Mother might entrust her orders to him or herself occupy a seat in the wagon.

Kindly Thomas Mills not only undertook to send his helper down with us to carry our purchases, but invited Mother first to come with him to inspect the boarding house. As the miners were all at work, we found the kitchen to be the only room occupied, and here three Chinese cooks were busily preparing the dinner to be served at noon. (This service was an unusual feature of this mine made possible by the boarding house's proximity to the entrance into the underground workings.) Already the baking of the day's bread was finished, and a great array of loaves, uniform in size and symmetry, all beautifully browned and smelling most appetizing, won Mother's admiration and her questions.

She was never to succeed in eliciting a crumb of information as to how this perfection was achieved but the cooks were pleased and even invited us to look through the door into their private apartment, the walls of which were adorned with brightly colored representations of ancestors and deities.

The kitchen was lined with cooking ranges and tables, each range polished and shining, each table scrubbed white, as was the bare floor. Each man wore his hair wound neatly round his head in a long braid since it was long before the time when queues would be cut from Chinese heads. I recall the name of only one of these skillful cooks, Dai Li (pronounced by us Daily), the one who was to remain longest in the company's employ and become an attached friend of our family.

Our arrival on the mountain added a third to the two families in residence there. Mother could not expect many callers, but she was not surprised to be greeted on this afternoon by Mrs. James, bringing with her the youngest of her four sons, little George. There was already a bond between the two women in Mrs. James's mother, Mrs. Richards, who had been one of Mother's best friends in Grass Valley. Brother and I soon received permission to amuse ourselves outside, with the stipulation that we remain within sight of the house.

Alas! it took only a brief walk along the horizontal trail to lead me into trouble, for I came upon a mud puddle, the sight of which sufficed to arouse in me a passion (long dormant) for the manufacture of mud pies. Down I sat, oblivious of my clean garments, and my freshly ironed dress was soon disgracefully soiled. This trifling incident remains in my memory as the occasion of the last corporal punishment ever inflicted on me by my mother and of the dawn in me of a new sense of responsibility, following the impact of a little switch in the hands of my usually so patient parent.

It was indeed time, my mother realized, to call upon her children for more help in these new, more primitive conditions. To me, who had already learned to make beds, was entrusted the washing of dishes after each meal. To Brother fell the chore of keeping Mother's wood box filled with stove-length logs, which Father had sawn from the pile in the yard.

On Father's band practice nights, he would leave them outside for Brother to carry into the woodshed at the end of the lean-to, and I think he never knew how Mother and I would make a game of joining Brother in this activity. Fun at first, these tasks were not easy to keep up day after day, when play was calling us out into the wonderful world of the mountainside. Of the two delinquents, I was the worse, often slipping away after a meal, leaving behind my unwashed dishes. My only punishment would be to find them awaiting me on my return — always they were there!

With Mrs. James as guide, we accompanied Mother to such points of interest as the carpenter shop at the end of the wagon road, the No. 7 quartz mill just below in the Buttes Ravine, and a waterfall higher up.

From a point on the flume above, on the boarding house level, we glimpsed several of the 14 arrastras, whose eerie shrieks had reached our ears mingled with the sound of the wind and the roar of the mill. They were strategically placed along the sides of the steeply descending Buttes Ravine, and were used to process the tailings which had passed through the mill.

In its earlier days the mine had been worked entirely by means of these Mexican forerunners of the stamp mill. As described by Rodman W. Paul, in his book, *California Gold*, the arrastra was developed in Spanish America:

> . . . to supply the need for a machine that was extremely simple in construction . . . To build it, flat-surfaced stones were fastened into a circular track, around which a low retaining wall was attached, like the arm on an old-fashioned marine windlass. Heavy abrasive stones were then placed in the track and connected to the shaft by long

ropes or chains. A mule, plodding in a perpetual circle, provided the power to put the stones in motion, so that the gold-bearing material would be ground between them and the flat-surfaced bed.

A similar device, known as the Chile mill, substituted a heavy stone wheel for the abrasives.

We had paused on the flume near a well-trodden trail leading upward through a grove of tall trees, which Mrs. James called sugar pines.[3] Mother paused to load me with some of the fallen cones and to gather some beautiful moss from the north side of these big trees. She lamented the general bareness of the mountain side, with only scattered small groves where she had expected to find a forest.

Mrs. James agreed, but more than 30 years of mining, with many miles of timber-devouring tunnels, had taken

Buttes Ravine arrastra

heavy toll from the original forest cover. It was fortunate, she thought, that in later years decision had been made to cut trees from the west side of the hill, sparing those about the mine buildings, and now a younger growth was springing up to repair the damage.

Our return journey was broken by a rest in Mrs. James' home, one of two comfortable houses built along the flume at some distance from the boarding house. With apologies for her housekeeping, she explained that her good maid had recently left her, and that she thought it hopeless to try to replace her until the new house which the company was building for them in Sierra City should be ready for occupancy. Lack of society on the "hill" made it almost impossible to persuade a girl to remain there. Mother sympathized, but must have felt the contrast between this roomy, attractively furnished two-story house and her own new quarters.

Disregarding everything else, my eyes fastened themselves upon some well-filled book shelves, and, to my great delight, Mrs. James added a volume of *Chatterbox* to the favorite novels she was selecting for Mother's perusal. Her son, Tom, was enlisted to help carry the load, which included a pail of strong beef-tea which passed for soup in Mrs. James' richly supplied kitchen.

Our introduction into the society at No. 7 was completed the following Sunday when Father presented his family to Superintendent Thomas Preston in his residence, the office of the Buttes Mine. A bachelor, he lived here with three clerical workers and Wong, his Chinese cook. The mine, being owned by a London company, had followed an English practice of employing as superintendent a business manager who was not a miner.

A Cornishman, Mr. James was responsible to Mr. Preston for operation of the mine and direction of its working force of miners. In effect, however, it was a division of authority, and might not have worked so well had not the mine been placed under the general supervision of a general manager with office in San Francisco. (William Johns was also an experienced miner, former superintendent of the great Plumas Eureka Mine at Johnsville in Plumas County.)

Mr. Preston seemed to like children and to take pleasure in showing us the retort furnace, in which the amalgam scraped from concentrators in the two mills was melted in order to separate the gold from the quicksilver. There, for the first time, we saw gold bricks fresh from the furnace. These were much larger than ordinary bricks and varied in color from palest gold to a deeper, reddish hue.

When Mr. Preston told us what they were worth (a fortune to a poor person) and said I might have the smallest brick if I could lift it, I tried with all my might, but of course I could not do. It was also my first sight of Norwegian skis, which Snowshoe Thomson had introduced into the Sierra, but Mr. Preston called them snowshoes, and in Sierra County we never heard them called by any other name.

In the evening of this eventful Sunday Mrs. James escorted us to the concert held in the boarding house every second and third Sunday, when there would be no church service. Like their Welsh cousins, Cornish miners could sing, and there were some skilled musicians among them, but of this evening's performance I recall only one solo, "Come Where My Love Lies Dreaming."

Our acquaintance with Tom James, but two or three years older than me, ripened in the next few weeks into something resembling tolerance on his part, which later became a real liking for Brother. Sometimes accompanied by an older brother, Will, he led us to some of the choicer play spots in the vicinity, chiefly the barn, a short distance below our own house. It was large with a second story filled with hay, and the road was extended on one side to form a good-sized "flat," covered by "spiling," a term at first unknown to us, and, perhaps, all new to you, dear reader? (It simply means piles or heaps of anything.) In this case, it was piles of lumber and of large iron pipes, nothing more; but can you think of a better place to play hide-and-seek?

At any rate, that is what we played there. Stationed in and about the barn were several cats, among them some charming kittens, whom we vainly tried to tame by offering food. They seemed as completely wild as were the chipmunks, which abounded on the mountain.

The large watering trough in front of the barn was found to contain several worms. Tom assured us they were simply transformed horse-hairs. He also affirmed that Jesus, whom we watched as he passed to and from with his mules, was "as old as the hills." As if this were not wonder enough, he pointed to the rocks looming above us on the mountain top and informed us that this whole Sierra Buttes mountain on which we were standing was just an extinct volcano and might burst out again like Vesuvius. I knew what a volcano was, for I had read about Pompeii in a travel book in our home library.[4] We would now always feel a little fearful when we looked up at our old man on the mountain.

Was life in our little house on the mountain as happy for Mother as she made it for her children? Among some letters which she always kept, I quote from one written by my beloved Aunt Minnie in Pennsylvania:

Dear Sadie:

I am sorry you are homesick and lonesome. I pray for you. I would not *dare* question in regard to all the ways our dear Heavenly Father has been permitting you to pass through. He knows best what is needed to perfect us . . . All things work together for good to those who love the Lord.

Another letter from this dear aunt is dated Nov. 6, 1885.

In Wyoming (Pa.) a few days in work for the Lord . . . The Salvation Army are still holding their meetings. God has blessed their work and will . . . they are fulfilling the word of God in Luke 14:23. They truly go out quickly in the streets . . . A word to dear children, dear Mabel and Willard. Aunt Minnie sends you mittens, good thick ones to keep your hands warm to play out in the cold wind, as Mama writes the wind blows so hard on the high mountain; also to bring in wood for Mama. I suppose you can work a little like good children to help Mama and Papa. I trust you remember Aunt Minnie when you pray to gentle Jesus night and morning. I remember you. Every night and morning I ask Jesus to keep you well and good.

God bless you.
Aunt Minnie.

Aunt Minerva's mittens were not the only precursors of winter. Mother's knitting needles were flying on little pairs of woolen stockings for Brother and me, and all too soon came that first cold day in November where we were obliged most unwillingly to don them, together with shirts and long drawers of red flannel, indeed a minor tragedy! Protest and tears were unavailing. The wool might be prickly, the flannel harsh to tender skins, but these must be our wear until late spring brought warmer days.

In the meantime, autumn days in the mountain's rarefied air were often clear and sparkling, and happy hours were spent in raising the log walls of our playhouse in the yard. As we learned our way up and down the trails, we found a treasure trove — nails, board for our roof, sacks to line the walls and toys for indoor play, like the cigar-box which became a coach for my paper dolls. With a sack and a small hatchet we ventured down the wagon road, scanning the hillsides for stumps which might contain the pitch pine needed for home fires.

Except on Sundays, when our activities were limited to sedate walks down the road with parents, the mountain was our playground. We shared it only with the pigs who were allowed to roam freely on the supposition that they kept the rattlesnakes under control and we only caught occasional glimpses of Jesus and the mules of Tom Williams and the team.

Six days in the week, the miners would be underground from 7 a.m. to 12 noon and again from 1 p.m. to 6 p.m. Promptly at noon they could be seen filing up the trail from No. 6 to the boarding house for the midday meal. By this time, we were expected to be at home to eat our own

Sierra Buttes miners with their meal buckets. Date unknown. *Thomas Family Photo*

dinners, but we often lingered at a point which commanded a view of the full length of this trail to witness a line of waiting men extending from a bend in the trail down to the mouth of the tunnel from which the miners had emerged. The sound of the 12 o'clock whistle would set all in motion, bring into full view those nearest the turn, followed by all the rest, marching swiftly in single file. Breaking the monotony of our day this sight always fascinated us.

I was for some months doomed to loneliness as the only girl on the mountain among six boys. Mrs. James' oldest son was away at school, and Will and Tom, her second and third, were both older than 5-year-old Brother. Perhaps they too were lonely, for they graciously allowed Brother and me to accompany them to various points of interest.

Under their escort we dared to invade the big barn, turning somersaults on the hay in the second floor, and

Sierra Buttes miners relaxing on a day off, dressed in their best clothes. *Courtesy of the Sierra County Historical Society*

playing hide and seek among the piles of lumber and iron pipes stored on the flat around it. We were once hard put to extricate little Tom Williams, who had made the error of crawling too far into one of these pipes.

Our most distant venture, which must have been attended by some risk, was a walk along the flume, or ditch, which brought the mine's water supply down from lakes seven miles distant on the other side of the mountain. There were occasional gaps in the planking and obstacles in the form of large storage tanks, in which we could easily have drowned. There was also the likelihood of meeting with rattlesnakes, which would have terrified me, but which I was given to understand, would be to the James boys merely a welcome diversion. Did my parents ever learn of this excursion? I do not know, but it had since occurred to me that they would not have approved of it.

But was not Christmas on the way, and Thanksgiving Day too? For these feasts there were great preparations to be made, in which Brother and I could join in helping Mother. How delicious was the aroma from the large pan of spiced pears simmering all day on the back of the kitchen range, and what fun it all was — seeding raisins, "stoning" currants, paring apples, beating eggs and chopping all the ingredients for mincemeat! Would Santa Claus find us here so far away on the mountain? How would he know that we were here? We need not have worried. He did find us in the little cabin, and his pack was not empty.

It was indeed a Christmas never to be forgotten. We were invited to one of Mrs. James' famous holiday dinners. Of her Christmas of the preceding year, the following account is quoted:

"Christmas was celebrated in regal style on the Buttes . . . Captain James set all at ease with the injunction, 'At Christmas play and make good cheere, for Christmas comes but once a yeare.' T.P. Williams replied for the guests happily and facetiously, with an account of the origin of the Christmas tree and ascribing customs in other countries especially in merrie England, ending with the role of Santa Claus in the 'newer brighter, greater, and happier Britain in America.' Later came recitations by Charley, Willie, and Tommy, and there were charades, dialogues, and tableaux by Mrs. and Miss Black, Miss Hobby and Messers Pierce, Black, Schutz and Pettingale. Presents were distributed and delicious refreshments served by Mrs. James. Twas voted by all a most wonderful Christmas party."

Not all of the same guests were present at our party, but our host greeted us with the same centuries-old Christmas couplet, and the feast set before us could not have been more abundant in the year preceding. T.P. Williams was there as well as another of the mines' local preachers, Brother George, and the latter's trip back to "the old country," projected for the following summer, was evidently a matter of lively interest in the assembled company, most of them natives of Cornwall.

"T.P.," one of the youngest among them, joined with eagerness in the discussion. I, of course, was too young to sense a mystery in the superior education and manifest abilities of this youthful miner. In the files of the *Downieville Messenger*[5] is a record of his lectures in that town on "Civilization of the Renaissance" and on "Eminent Cornishmen" (subject of a book he has written).

That paper also notes his participation in a philosophical disputation, printing at length his reply (under the pseudonym "Percival") to the heretical opinions of one calling himself "Iconoclast." [6] We learn, too, of T.P.'s engagement by the Republican Central Committee to "canvass the northern counties" in the political campaign of 1886.[7]

Heavy winter snowfall meant hours of fun on sleds and snowshoes for children in Sierra City. *Courtesy of the Sierra County Historical Society*

CHAPTER 5

Snowshoes and Sleigh Bells

Our first winter on the mountain would be remembered
having one of the heaviest winds in years.[1] It blew
in January, strong enough to move the No. 7 boarding
house a foot from its foundation, despite the great timbers
supporting it. It blew smoke down our chimney in such
volume that Mother would make us lie down on the floor,
lest we be smothered.

The snow it brought was deep enough to carry away a
section of the flume leading down from the lakes, obliging
us to melt snow to obtain the water we used. Men were
diverted from the mine to rid roofs of the snow which
threatened to crush them. Snow crystals made pictures on
our windows, and hanging from every roof were long icicles,
thick as a man's arm. Miners walked to work clad in rubber
hip boots. I remember "nips" (flannel cloths) in which Father
wrapped his feet to keep them warm inside the cold rubber.

The stages to and from Downieville and Sierra City
were still running, although at a snail's pace, using sleighs
drawn by horses mounted on snowshoes.[2] Except for violent
winds, which kept the air so full of snow that it was difficult
to breathe, the mountains had seen far worse winters. Four

years earlier, one seven-week storm had left 5 feet of snow in Sierra City, 18 to 20 inches at Gold Lake, and 12 inches at Mountain House which was the same altitude as No. 7.[3]

That storm of 1882 had brought avalanches in Buttes Ravine, which damaged most of the arrastras there, swept away the old Hanks Mill, and badly wrecked the large Hitchcock Mill just below it. As a result of these slides, 100 men were for a time out of work at the mine.

It was deemed fortunate that our winter of 1886 brought no greater disaster than the speedily repaired damage to the flume. The snow was spaced at intervals which permitted us children to coast down the steep trail leading to the boarding house and down to the barn. As sun appeared to soften the snow, skis (always called snowshoes by us) became the chief means of locomotion, and men were set to clear some few paths in the snow for those who ventured out without them.

Brother was soon mounted on a diminutive pair and learning to compound his own "dope," a lubricant made from a formula given to him by the James boys. Melted to the right consistency on the back of our stove, it was applied to the bottom of the snowshoes to increase their speed.[4]

From early January to mid-March, the mountain was covered by snow and we were confined to the house save for brief excursions up or down the few trails kept open by the men. On very windy days, we were practically prisoners. Mrs. James, venturing out one afternoon to call on Mother, declared she had been lifted off her feet by the wind, and had, for a moment, feared she would be blown away.

Except for our morning coasting or skiing, we children remained in the house, where we found much to occupy us, either in play or in "helping Mother" in the little ways she contrived to keep us busy. Although our most boisterous games were permitted only in our own room at the opposite end of the house from Mother's, we were, when very good, admitted to play quietly in her room, where she might be using the sewing machine in manufacture of family apparel. I remember Brother's lead soldiers, two sets of them, one in British red, the other in American blue and buff, and I still see Father's rueful smile as he watched the redcoats (his countrymen) soundly beaten.

Outstanding in memory is that day on which Brother was promoted out of his small boys' attire of kilts into his first pair of small trousers. Was there a suspicion of tears in Mother's eyes as she watched him bounding back and forth across the room and shouting in a very ecstasy of glee?

It was indeed a very great day, one fit to be celebrated by a molasses-candy pull. The candy was prepared on our versatile wood range by boiling the mixture down to the right consistency for pulling. As this was an exercise in which any number and all ages could engage, it was a favorite party amusement of that day, but was not too difficult for our small party of three, and how handy it was to have, just outside on the stoop, plenty of snow to cool the syrup!

Much as she had to do, Mother found ways as she cooked, washed and sewed for her small household, to amuse us when we wearied of toys within and of watching the storm clouds without. We played games, from "Simon says, Thumbs up!" to "Hunt the Thimble," or "Hide and Go Seek," or "Pussy Wants a Corner," and sometimes Mother would read aloud or tell a story. Most of all we liked to help her cook, and what fun it was, when the snow was falling outside on the stoop, to gather some and make "ice cream" by mixing it with milk and sugar.

Our greatest resource was Mrs. James' library and her generosity in lending its books. For a short time after our arrival, Brother and I were among the pupils whom Mr. James had arranged should be taught by that brilliant young miner, T.P. Williams.

When we lost this good teacher, Mother was obliged to add to her duties that of our instruction in reading, writing, arithmetic and geography. Beginning with the alphabet, Brother seemed to learn as painlessly as I had done while reading my way through publications of the American Tract Society from the Sunday School I attended in Grass Valley. At any rate, he was soon reading the rhymes in our copy of *Mother Goose Melodies*. (It must have been a New England edition for he often sang, as he rode on Father's foot, "Trot, trot to Boston; Trot, trot to Lynn, Trot, Trot to Concord; And trot back again.")

Reading and play alike were interrupted by childhood ailments. We were yet to hear of influenza, but colds predominated and Mother was our physician. Her faith in homeopathic remedies abounded, and her medicine case was filled with little bottles of diminutive pills, aconite, nux vomica, and many others she administered according to instructions on the labels. Invariably sweet and pleasant to taste, we much preferred them to the bowls of hot drinks which she brewed from herbs, most of them bitter and strong of flavor. (One of these I recall as made of mullein leaves, another of elderberry blossoms.)

We suffered most from the plasters, which, upon the first symptom of congestion, she would apply to our chests.

They contained an irritant in effect similar to that of the mustard which she reserved for her more desperate cases. She bandaged stiff necks with cloths soaked in kerosene, which also served as an irritant. For hoarseness she made a syrup from onions baked with sugar. For a conscientious objector to onion, she might consent to substitute lemons.

Our tortures were mitigated by the special dainties she considered suitable invalid fare, beef tea, poached eggs on toast made over the coals and well buttered, or an eggnog, flavored with vanilla or with a dash of brandy and a sprinkling of nutmeg. Taking everything into consideration, illness was a luxury when Mother was our nurse.

The housewife of the 1880s had never heard of appliances; her cook stove had no fuel other than wood or coal, and the household water heater, if any, was an appendage of that same stove. We, of course, at No. 7 had none, the cold water piped into the lean-to being our sole convenience.

Washday, always a Monday, was one of intense activity. Before the 6 o'clock breakfast, Father would help by bringing from the lean-to three heavy wooden tubs, together with the benches which supported them. The wash boiler would be mounted across the front of the stove with a sufficient quantity of the soapy water in which the white clothes would be boiled. If in those days there existed such a thing as soap powder, we never heard of it. Liquid soap or detergents were also unknown. Mother took a knife to shave from the soap bar the amount required.

It took time to bring that boilerful of clothes to a boil, but Mother need not be idle. There was the problem of all the woolen things and all the colored things, which could not be boiled and must be cleansed by sturdy rubbing on a washboard. It consisted of crosswise metal cleats, against which the clothes were rubbed up and down. If you tried it, you might find it exhausting before morning's end. Naturally, I was soon drafted to lend aid, from which Brother's sex and tender years alike exempted him.

A 19th century ironing day is pictured in The Kingdom of Home, an 1888 book of poems about the home.

Two tubs were filled, one with warm, the other with cold water. From the rubbing tub, the clothes progressed in order first white, then colored, into the rinsing tub, then into the bluing tub. Some of the cotton things and all the woolen things were done.

The other things were starched before hanging them up to dry. Mother made her starching by boiling flour in water, to which traditionally there was added a pinch of salt and a morsel of butter. I would keep stirring this mixture as it boiled, and a little more salt would be added in the tears which fell into it as I stirred. If all went well, and it would be contingent on the weather, Tuesday was normally devoted to ironing the results of Monday's labor.

The facilities of our all-duty kitchen were not inferior to the average home of the day. There was no such thing as an electric iron, only a number of heavy objects called sadirons which were heated on top of the kitchen range; and on the mountain, there was no commercial laundry to which could be shifted the task of ironing Father's white shirts and our better cotton dresses.

Whatever the weather, a hot fire must be kept up on ironing day, which was also one of the week's two or three baking days. Sierra City never boasted a bakery; all the bread, pies, and cakes were necessarily homemade, even to the yeast that went into the bread. Each day there were three meals to be prepared, and all dishes — soups, puddings, pies and cakes — were cooked without benefit of any of the ready mixes and powders available today.

In my memory of this winter, books seem to predominate over play. It was then that Louisa Alcott came into my life through a copy of her *Little Women* sent to me by Aunt Minerva. This delightfully natural tale of wholesome family life may have served as an antidote to my reading of several novels of fashionable London society by "The Duchess" lent by Mrs. James to Mother.

Before she was aware that I was reading them, Father made the shocking discovery. "She will be ruined!" he exclaimed, and "The Duchess" was banished from our house.

From my perusal of her works I retain only an image of her heroines, always dazzlingly beautiful and seeming always to be arrayed either in black velvet with pearls or in white satin with diamonds.

Jane Porter's *Scottish Chiefs* and her *Thaddeus of Warsaw* moved me far more, but it was her heroes, depicted as paragons of valor and virtue, not her heroines, who impressed me. I do not deny that I greatly admired Miss Porter's works, but I cannot now disagree with an opinion of her biographer: "Her historical novel, *The Scottish Chiefs*, found many admirers, but it is very defective as a delineation of character and manners." Nevertheless I do not count as wasted the time spent in reading it, for it awakened an interest in history which has persisted through the years. I found, too, in an old textbook of Mother's, an account of Mary, Queen of Scots, and in one of Mrs. James' magazines a story of Joan of Arc. I wept when my parents could not answer all my questions.

I did read one truly great book that winter, John Bunyan's *Pilgrim's Progress*, which Father had brought, together with his Bible, from home and had carried with him through all his hardships and far journeys. Of Bunyan's book Lord Macaulay wrote, "We are not afraid to say that, although there were many clever men in England during the latter half of the 17th century, there were only two great creative minds. One of these minds produced *Paradise Lost* and the other, the *Pilgrim's Progress*."

Mrs. James' *Chatterbox* was followed by several annual volumes of *Harper's Young People*, from which Mother read aloud to Brother and me. We especially delighted in the old fairy tales, inimitably retold and illustrated by Howard Pyle. Had there been comic books for children then, could we have enjoyed them so much? Perhaps so, but I doubt if they could have enriched our memories as did these volumes, the work of some of the (18)80s best writers and artists.

The Dec. 1, 1885 cover of the *Harper's Young People*, probably read to Mabel and Willard Thomas by their mother

A vintage postcard shows summertime on the Sierra Buttes.

CHAPTER 6

Summertime
on the Mountain

April came; and the sun having melted all the snow, the streams and waterfalls were full, spring flowers were blooming and new leaves appearing on deciduous trees and shrubs, while on all the evergreen trees every branch and branchlet showed fresh tips of lighter hue. The sun shone warm on our southern slope of the mountain, and all around life seemed springing, while the sky above was a glory of shining clouds against the intense blue.

After winter's monotonous whiteness, Mother found the change almost too exciting for her children, who longed to wander freely about in this wonderful new world, and at first restricted us to an area near the house where there was a thicket of tall shrubs. Brother discovered that climbing up into one of them gave some semblance to riding a horse. Soon we were bouncing up and down on our respective steeds, Brother on "Young Lollard," I on "Black Bess."[1] Employment of these gallops may have led to some tree climbing, for I recall spending much of our summer seated in comfort with a book among the upper branches of a tall black oak.

But soon the house across the trail was no longer empty, and I was no longer the only girl on the mountain. In February, Emil Schutz had returned to his former post as millwright, in charge of the carpenter shop at the end of the road overlooking the No. 7 mill; and now his wife and four children had arrived to be our neighbors. This event, exciting for Brother and me, was not less welcome to Mother, who had been sadly anticipating her loneliness on the early removal of Mrs. James to her new house in the city below. The second of the boys was little older than Brother, while Lulu, the oldest of the two girls although younger than I, soon became a beloved companion, with little Pauline toddling along between us in most of our undertakings.

I could no longer count on Brother always to participate since he was sometimes permitted to join in some activity of the older boys. They played games like prisoners' base or at being Indians on the warpath; they played with balls and with slingshots and bows and arrows, from any of which Brother might come running, with some minor injury, to Mother to be bandaged and comforted.

Fired by their reading of one of Mrs. James' books, *The Swiss Family Robinson*, the boys had constructed, some distance above ground in the branches of a tall oak tree, a playhouse roomy enough to accommodate all six of them in its leafy shelter, but at which we three girls, not being invited to climb up, could only gaze in wistful admiration. Alas for their scornful superiority when that tree house came tumbling down, and with it all six boys! To the general amazement, the resulting damage was limited to superficial cuts and bruises.

Meantime, we girls had set up housekeeping in a pine grove by a sparkling little brook, which, with its adjacent maples, was a joy to see. Conveniently located not far below the barn, it was well secluded from any of the trails. With our thick carpet of pine needles, our shady roof of pine, fir, and cedar branches, and our garden of ferns beside the pretty, gurgling brook we no longer felt any need of tree houses.

We played with dolls, I with two relics of younger days, Olive a wax doll from Germany, and Violet, a bisque baby doll from France. But we vastly preferred some paper dolls I had cut from colored fashion plates in discarded numbers of Mrs. James' "Young Ladies' Journal," published in London. These were appropriately christened from characters in the Duchess' novels, and I laboriously inscribed a name on the back of each doll. They lived in a little moss-covered house made by Mother, and we drew them about in a carriage which had once served as a cigar box. (Was not the coach in which Cinderella rode made out of a pumpkin?)

The younger boys joined us in sailing boats on the little brook, but our happiest days were those on which we set out on some tour of exploration up or down the mountain. Perhaps we might discover a slope covered with wild flowers new to us, and we found one day a spot on which wild onions grew. We pulled them up and carried them home to patient Mother, who was not too busy to set out plates with seasoning of vinegar and salt, a feast for our small company.

Below the buildings, there were the road and two trails leading to No. 8: one for pedestrians, the other for timber, along which we might meet Jesus driving his two mules.

A 1913 botanical drawing of a wild
onion, from *The Illustrated Flora of
the Northern States and Canada*

We usually chose the road because it was less steep and commanded wider views. The first mile led westward to Ladies'
Canyon, a vast depression, at which our road forked, one
branch swerving to the east and leading down to Sierra City.
The other climbed northerly up the steep side of the canyon, past the Colombo and Independence mines, and past
a junction with a road to Whitney's Timber Camp, which
connected to a trail to the Buttes summit. From where we
stood, we could follow the steady progress of our main road
as it veered farther to the northwest and until it disappeared
over the top of the ridge, on its way to Butcher's Ranch.

The turn of the road from which we viewed all this was
called Cape Horn. Odd names, you think? Yes, but there is
even worse to tell. Another lovely canyon, near neighbor to

Ladies', was (and still is) known as Hog Canyon, and over on the mountain's north side, not far below the craggy summit of the Buttes, are two of the most beautiful small lakes in all California, which appear on all the maps under the names, Upper and Lower Sardine.[2] Surely the men of the Fifties have much to answer for!

Did we walk this way so many times to admire the scenery? I am sure we had no such thought. Nevertheless, it did something to us — something we began to feel even in the year following, upon our going to live in the town below. Just as our Father would never forget the Cornish sands and cliffs over which he roamed as a boy, so Brother and I would carry always with us an ache of homesickness for these mountains on which we were so happily playing.

On Sundays, we soberly walked this road with our parents. There was no racing back and forth, no climbing some of the huge rocks which towered above it. Our Sunday clothes would have hampered us, even had there been no grown persons along.

The exception was a weekday when Mrs. Schutz and Mother accompanied us down the same road to a trail not far from Cape Horn that led down to a mountain meadow, screened by trees from the road above. A little stream meandered alongside, and on it grew the watercress which was the object of our expedition. It was, however, forgotten in the surprise and wonder of finding three deserted cabins bordering the meadow, obviously the encampment of some long-vanished miners. We saw no visible evidence of mining operation, nothing save the cabins, empty and falling into ruin, and the watercress (not native to California).

"The Cups," Mrs. Schutz called the place, but the origin of the name she did not know.[3]

Watercress and onions were not the only crops we harvested as summer ripened such fruits as grew on the mountainside. Most abundant were elderberries and cherries, both of them promising in appearance but disappointing to taste. The "choke cherries," as we called the acrid fruit, we never put to any use, but Mother produced really good elderberry pies by judiciously mixing some of the green fruit with the ripe. Gooseberries, despite their armor of prickly thorns, were converted into jelly, as were the wild plums, which grew in scattered locations and were sought by camping parties from as far as Sierra Valley.

Even more eagerly we children searched for a wild raspberry, which grew along the ditches and resembled the "black-caps" we had known in Pennsylvania. Here we had to proceed with care, fearing rattlesnakes, but encountered none, although Brother, venturing too near a yellow jacket's nest, was severely stung. It may have been deserved reprisal for the number of the nests we destroyed during the summer. They seemed to be everywhere, invading the houses in such swarms that no one escaped being stung many times.

After flowing through seven miles of flumes, our drinking water arrived at a temperature more than tepid, and we greatly enjoyed our daily pilgrimages, carrying demijohns to be filled with icy water flowing (from some submerged "glacial remnants") out of the mouth of the disused No. 5 tunnel. Grandmother in Pennsylvania would surely have approved our being so usefully employed, one of her favorite proverbs being, "Satan will find mischief still for idle hands to do."

Alas that we could not always be busy and, in our play, could not always agree. Quarrels would arise, not only among the boys, but between Lulu and me, when her high spirit caused her to rebel against the leadership I, as the elder, would arrogate to myself. In a clash of wills, we might part in anger to mount our respective fences, thence to hurl insults at each other until overheard by one or both of our mothers. What then happened to Lulu I do not know, but I would be banished to my lonely room, there to meditate until I had "asked God to make me a good little girl."

On my emergence at length in penitent mood, Mother would greatly point out that I was responsible for the younger children, and that kind Mrs. Schutz thought that I was always taking good care of Lulu and Pauline, and see-ing that they came to no harm. "Little birds in their nests agree," Mother would say, always ending with her hope that someday I might learn to be a lady.

It was, perhaps, on one such melancholy day that, walk-ing alone up the trail, I chanced to meet that great man, Superintendent Preston. He stopped me with a smile, and (having evidently forgotten my name) with the kindly inquiry, "Do you like sweets?"

Embarrassed, for I had never heard, nor in my reading ever met, with this word, "sweets," I blurted out the only answer which came to mind: "No."

I did not see the expression with which he so quickly turned away, but I had taken but few steps before my slug-gish wits had associated the new word with those boxes of candy for which Brother spent the coins so frequently bestowed upon him by men he met in Father's company. I possessed nothing of the social grace, the savoir faire, which would have enabled me to run after Mr. Preston with an apology. I was unable to confess my blunder even to Mother.

Brother, too, was concealing one of his experiences, and with better reason, for it must assuredly have met with disapproval. Brother George[4] had returned from the old country, bringing with him a gift for brother, a toy flute. It had stops which could be worked, and on which, for a time, Brother practiced with much perseverance. But not for long although years passed before we learned why his interest so abruptly ceased.

It had begun with an illustration in *Chatterbox* of an Indian snake charmer at work. Would not such a picture rouse in any energetic boy an ambition to do likewise, especially if he were in a neighborhood where snakes were not uncommon? True, Brother's belief that we were in such a place, would, had they known of it, been met with contradiction from the officers of the Buttes Co., the herds of swine which freely roamed the mountainside being supposed by them to have eliminated all snakes from the mine's vicinity.

"Not so," Brother could have told them, but never did. For some time, he had been saving for this experiment a rattlesnake whose acquaintance he had made on the big flat back of the boarding house, and on the day when he thought himself to have acquired a degree of proficiency in tooting his small instrument, he stole off with it alone. Informing no one of his purpose, he made straight for the tall pine tree in which he knew the reptile made his or her home, arranged himself at what he thought a suitable distance, and began to play on all his stops. Did anything happen?

Yes, something did; as he used years later to tell it, "The snake stuck out his head, then drew it back and disappeared."

The tune must have not been to his liking, for he deigned no further notice of it. Much to Father's disappointment, Brother showed no further evidence of ambition for a musical career.

One of the joys of summer on the mountain was to watch the movement of rain clouds over the wide expanse of sky above and canyon below visible from our front windows. I am unable to explain what we so many times saw — a mist floating from the summit of the Buttes down over the surface of the mountain until it obscured the town and the river, thence rising to the top of the opposite range, where it reversed its course, returning down over the town, and back up to the peaks from which it had first seemed to appear.

A short distance down our wagon road was a small, rocky plateau, from which we had a fine view of buildings going up in the town beneath. Most interesting was the mansion erected for Mr. Watt Hughes, one of the six owners of the new Young America Mine. Mr. James' new house, too, was almost completed, and the stand in Buttes Park[5] for Father's band was ready in June. The band was now trained to what might be called concert pitch, often in summer evenings playing on our observation platform, from which they could be heard in Sierra City, and giving regular Sunday concerts from the new bandstand.

All, however, was not harmony in Sierra City that year. The dance houses, said the *Sierra Tribune*, were the source of much evil. Meetings of the miners' Anti-Chinese Association were being held in many places. There was only one in our town, however, and the local Chinese continued unperturbed to go about their own affairs in their own quiet way. Mainly, they worked over the streams and old abandoned mining claims, from which, now and then, news would leak of the discovery of some large nugget, which the white man had unaccountably overlooked. They were also the best cooks, and the eating places which discontinued their services incurred certain loss of patronage. But the men who ate in the Buttes Mine boarding house continued to enjoy their well-cooked meals.

All too soon it was September. Fall brought the menace of forest fires, and we were soon to have our first experience of one. It began near Loganville, a tiny settlement on the river, two miles below Sierra City by stage road and some 2,000 feet by trail from the Number 7 boarding house. From the summit of the ridge on which the Buttes Mine buildings were situated was a footpath leading down to Loganville and near the thickets of ripening wild plums[6] which attracted from far and near the campers whose carelessness was sometimes to blame for fires originating there.

The fire of 1886 may have smoldered for some time, and, lacking a favorable wind, we might never have heard of it; but when a strong northeast wind began to blow, driving the flames straight up the mountain, it gained such headway that, when the mine whistles did sound, it was to summon every man to fire duty. The older boys were pressed into service, leaving only Tom to act as messenger between the firefighters and the women and children.

The horses and mules were needed to carry supplies to the fire line, and we were instructed to prepare for evacuation on foot by the Sierra City trail. Mother began to collect the few necessities we might be able to carry, sandwiches, some articles of clothing, small pieces of her wedding silver. We had made ourselves as ready as we could when Tom

Prunus subcordata, the species of wild plum found in Sierra County. *Photo by Stan Shebs, Regional Parks Botanical Garden, Berkeley, California*

came with news that the fire was very close to the summit, and final word might soon come. The men would make a stand to save the buildings but we were not to wait for that. Mother said we should sit down and be very quiet.

Brother led us in a prayer. Just as when he said his daily evening prayer, he knelt at Mother's feet, asking "What shall I say, Mamma?" Now he repeated after her a short prayer that God would take care of all of us on the mountain and help the men to put out the fire.

We had not waited long when Tom came running, but this time he was shouting, "The wind has changed! The wind has changed!"

How happy we were then when we learned that all the men were safe and the buildings unharmed. The experience awakened us to the danger for forest fires, and the fear was to remain with us. Three years later, a far more disastrous fire, originating near Loganville, was to follow almost the same course up the mountain. (There was no Forest Lookout Station on the Buttes.)

Summer was the season when climbing parties scaled the peaks from various directions. Those coming from Sierra City had the advantage of our wagon road, leading them past Cape Horn on to its junction with the trail to the timber camp.

J.L. Wolfe recounts the following from an ascent in September 1932 to the Lookout Station:[7]

The Lookout starts us off on the trail up the final 600 feet to the top-most pinnacle. Both hands and feet are required to keep from tumbling down the dizzy sides and to the climber it seems as though, should he fall, he would not stop his tumbling until he had reached the bottom of the canyon, visible as a miniature a mile below. A particularly steep rocky slope is covered by a short ladder, and again we clamber from rock to rock until we reach the foot of a ladder extending about 40 feet up the last final perpendicular rock face. We climb the 22 rungs and have reached the top of this tremendous wind-swept pile of barren granite. Here, for more than a century, men have carved their names and the date in this everlasting rock. In the east, the first perpendicular drop is more than 1,200 feet. Then, a small glacier and the slope hurtle down to the three lakes. In all perhaps 20 lakes are visible, and on a clear day Mount Shasta and Mount Lassen pierce the northern horizons. The whole Sacramento Valley, the Lake County mountains, and the Pacific spread to the west; the chain of the Sierra Nevadas stretch down into the south, and the State of Nevada fades away into the east.

The Sierra Buttes Mine Band lines up before the bandstand on Busch's Flat. The date is unknown, but probably late 1880s. Stephen Thomas is on the far right, holding a trumpet. His son Willard is the boy on the left on the bandstand. The photo is taken by mining engineer William Letts Oliver. *Oliver Family Collection, Courtesy of The Bancroft Library, University of California, Berkeley*

CHAPTER 7

The Queen's Jubilee Caps a Year of Novelty

We had no idea that the fall of 1886 marked the peak of Sierra City's growth. The hamlet of 1863, nestling at the foot of the trail leading up to the big mine, had burgeoned over 25 years to this thriving town of the '80s.

Even if the Sierra Buttes Mine, after 30 years of bonanza, were to decline into "borrasca," there seemed no reason to fear it would diminish the swelling tide of prosperity flowing from other mines of the region. The Young America Mine seemed on the way to surpass the Buttes at its summit of production, while the Colombo, the Cleveland, the Marguerite, the Phoenix and many others had reached a paying stage.[1]

While hopes for the future of the Buttes Mine now centered about the No. 9 tunnel, the upper levels were by no means abandoned. Ore from No. 8 was still moving down the tramway to be crushed in the No. 9 mill, while the old Hitchcock mill was being refitted with stamps for ore left on dumps at still higher levels. At several outlying mines, the discovery of large nuggets was encouraging, the largest being reported by the Hayes and Steelman claim at Gold Lake. Mrs. James' oldest son, Charley, prospecting up the mountain with a partner, had taken up a promising claim near the old Independence mine, which they named the Gladstone.

All the good news, however, was counterbalanced by an order closing indefinitely all hydraulic mines on the north side, coupled with an injunction forbidding owners to sell water for hydraulicking.[2] For Sierra County, it was the beginning of the end of its most profitable form of mining. For a few years longer, in spite of mining spies, it would be surreptitiously carried on in remote canyons, but increasingly vigilant law enforcement rendered its suppression inevitable.

Sierra City's younger set was not depressed by the bad news. The Dancing Club was planning a masquerade ball, at which the Buttes band would play and two young miners would appear, one as the Earl of Leicester, the other as the Duke of Buckingham. Perhaps the ladies would be less splendid, one of them impersonating a snow storm, another the Buttes Mine. The versatile Charley James led a hunting party into Sierra Valley, returning with a bag of 400 rabbits, 30 sage hens, and two grouse. A skating ring, opened in December, enabled everyone to be gay, and surprise parties were numerous. Less innocent was the gambling pursued in the three dance houses and the many saloons.

Mrs. James would not spend another Christmas on the Hill, for, too soon for us, her house down the mountain would be ready for occupancy. Her departure deprived us of a good neighbor, but gave us a friend to visit in Sierra City; and Mother, with Brother and me, was early invited to stay overnight in the new house, where a Chinese cook reigned in the kitchen. There a system was soon arranged, via Tom Williams and his team, to continue our exchange of borrowed cooks.

The mine management — Superintendent Preston and his clerical force — had moved three months earlier than the James family into the new three-story office with its electrical lights, bathroom and sanitary plumbing.

I associate this period with *Uncle Tom's Cabin, Robinson Crusoe,* and replacing The Duchess' romantic novels with Rosa Carey's mild tales of English country life. It was also then that Brother and I encountered our first dime novel, gleaned from among the untidy discards strewn by the miners about the mountainside.

The Sierra Buttes Mine office as it looked in August 2010. It was completed in 1886 when the James family moved down here from No. 7. The Thomas family lived in the house in the 1890s after Stephen took over the mine management. *Thomas Family Photo*

A literary masterpiece, *The Unknown Marksman*, thrilled us by its succession of exciting episodes, where the lovely though unfortunate heroine was saved in the very nick of time by a sudden shot, aimed apparently from nowhere by a mysterious rifleman. The final pages of this enthralling narrative were missing and it was indeed a grievous sorrow, for the identity of the noble Unknown was forever a mystery.

Thanksgiving Day came and Mother cooked a turkey, but on the Hill was no service of thanks to signalize the day. Not long after, Mother received a caller, Mrs. Hockin, from Sierra City, bringing with her a small daughter, in whom I was delighted to see a girl of my own age.

"Oh, don't you love to read?" was my greeting, a most unfortunate one, for I was dismayed by the blank and almost frightened expression with which she recoiled from me.

It was my first intimation that joy in reading was not universal among children. The shock was considerable, and I did not repeat the error, when a year later, I met others of the juvenile population of Sierra City. I restricted my literary communication to storytelling, which Brother's interest had encouraged me to practice.

Mrs. Hockin's call anticipated an event of which Brother and I had no forewarning, the coming to our house of a baby brother. Had we known of it, we might have enjoyed the pleasures of anticipation, but, in accordance with the custom of that time, it was denied us. So it befell that it was not altogether a pleasant surprise, when, on the morning of Dec. 9, we awakened to find no Mother in the living room, only a new baby in the cradle we had never seen, and Mrs. Hockin in charge.

The night of Dec. 8 had been stormy, and Father had been obliged to make his way down the trail to Sierra City in order to see that doctor and nurse were safely conveyed by carriage up the wagon road. There had fortunately been a physician in town, which was by no means always the case. Dr. Tully had recently been appointed Buttes Mine medical officer, making two doctors resident in town.

There was no hospital nearer than Downieville, but no sick miner was ever left to languish alone in his solitary cabin. Nursing was a community responsibility, and there was no Board of Health even in Downieville, the county seat. Friends and neighbors would divide among them the care of an invalid, and miners, all working their 10 hours a day, never hesitated to take each their share of the burden; for this no compensation was expected, nor would have been accepted, had it been offered.

No sister could have been kinder to Mother than was good Mrs. Schutz, helping to plan our meals, and adding the burden of our marketing to her own. Mother was indeed very ill, and Mrs. Hockin was still with us to prepare the Christmas dinner.

The yellow jacket plague had led to predictions of hard winter. Father had scorned the idea: "Poor silly fools." But now, as January storms were prolonged through February, Brother and I began to wonder if the yellow jackets had not been right, after all.

A storm from Feb. 5 to 19 was pronounced by the *Messenger* to be the heaviest since 1850. For two weeks, no stage came through from below, and what mail and express was received had been carried on skis by way of the river. The roughest storm of all, with very high winds, came on

Feb. 26. In Downieville next morning the snow was 4 feet deep and the mercury at 6 degrees above zero.

It was worse on the mountain, and Brother's snowshoe "dope" became a fixture on the back of the stove. While he delighted in daily practice on his skis, I was proud to be helping Mother by minding the baby, rocking him in a quaint wooden cradle, shaped long before by some handy miner, and previously occupied by several other infants born upon the mountain.

While little Arthur slept, I had time to read, perched on his high chair, my book supported before me on its convenient shelf. It was there, with snow falling outside the windows, that I began my reading of the King James Bible, calling now and then for Mother's help on some difficult name. I read that winter most of the narrative books of the Old Testament. A little book of Bible stories had carried me from Adam and Eve to the fall of Jericho, where it abruptly terminated. My sorrow at this disappointment induced Mother to give me the book itself and, with judicious skipping of genealogies and other dull passages, I found it entrancing.

Not until the middle of March did Mother venture out into the world, when already the snow was beginning to melt. We planned an expedition to the carpenter shop overlooking the mill. Mrs. Schutz, carrying the baby, sank down repeatedly onto the softening snow, to be extricated only by our combined efforts. The joy of being out in the sunshine was nevertheless so great that we persevered, and Mr. Schutz expedited our return by sending his helper to escort us.

Brother and I did not know that it would be our last winter on the mountain, nor could we have anticipated how durable and precious would be our memories of the life we lived there, on how many a storm-filled night we would be carried back to the feelings of warmth, of safety and of love which made that little house a home.

But there remained for us a second glorious summer on the mountain. We were no longer content with childish games like hide-and-seek. While Lulu and I spent days in lacing together a fantastically long chain of pine needles, reaching from our house to Schutzes', the boys were shaping a summer slide, beginning at the lower edge of the trail leading past the Schutz house, and extending down the vertical hillside almost to the edge of the wagon road. It was not the purpose to ski, but to coast, down this surface, which was so rough as to require slides of sturdier make than those used in winter.

With the help of some of their father's tools, the boys built slides of discarded lumber, with great perseverance using the finished sleds to smooth the slide's surface until it sparkled in the sun like glass and the sleds had become as speedy as any winter toboggan. The summer slide was a success, and a nine-day wonder to the adults who, with disparaging shaking of heads, had predicted its failure. Meanwhile, Lulu, Pauline and I had been far from disinterested spectators, coveting and getting sleds of our own and using them to contribute something to the final polishing of the slide's surface.

Tuesday, June 21, 1887, would long be remembered in Sierra City as the day we celebrated the Queen's Jubilee, the 50th anniversary of the reign of Queen Victoria over the British Empire. London kept the day by a solemn service in Westminster Abbey, to which the Queen went in state, "surrounded by the most brilliant royal and princely escort that had ever attended a British sovereign, and cheered on her way by the applause of hundreds of thousands of her subjects."

Superintendent Preston came to our house on a Sunday morning to broach his plan with Father to honor the great Queen. My father was not enthusiastic. With habitual plainness of speech, he made it clear that, as an American citizen, his participation in this program would be motivated by no sentiment of loyalty toward his former sovereign. Thomas Preston bore it well. Admirably detached, he outlined the musical details in every particular, and he knew that they would be carried out.

On the following Sunday, something of a sensation was created on our hill when our No. 7 ball team began playing cricket instead of baseball. We heard that it was by "royal decree," (Mr. Preston's). Excitement mounted still higher when word came that the opposing Sierra City team was likewise practicing the new game each evening and with the utmost assiduity. Down in the city, too, as the *Messenger* reported, was a Committee of Arrangements hard at work, soliciting "a large quantity of provisions for the picnic and money for the games." The exercises were "to commence as soon after nine o'clock as possible."

The festivities were held under the trees on Busch's Flat, where, at noon, a picnic lunch was to be served, followed by literary exercises and appropriate music from a platform erected for the purpose. But alas! The day was not blessed with "Queen's weather," and the afternoon program was cut short by an untimely shower.

Let the *Messenger* tell it:[3]

There were a large number of visitors present. Some came up from Grass Valley and a large number from Downieville and Goodyears. The cricketers played a game of cricket in which the No. 7 boys defeated the No. 8 and 9, after which lunch was served . . . It was voted the best laid table ever seen here. The only thing that marred the pleasure of the day was a shower during the afternoon which caused the Committee to dispense with the literary program. . . . The Sierra Buttes Band had favored us with some very fine music during the day. The children enjoyed themselves, playing games, riding the mule, racing etc. After which the majority of the folks left for their places of abode to prepare for the crowning event of the day: the fireworks, which were the best ever seen in Sierra City. The whole event was concluded with a social dance.

Perhaps our regret for the unfinished program is keener than was that of those present that afternoon. It is certain that "Rule Britannia" would have been well rendered by the Buttes' best baritone, and most of the audience, even the school children, could have joined in singing "God Save the Queen," since most of those who did not know the words of that song were familiar with the song of "America" and the tunes were the same.

The Thomas family in an 1887 photo taken in the Andrew Price studio in Sierra City. From left to right: Sarah with baby Arthur on her lap, Mabel, age 9; Stephen and Willard, age 7. *Thomas Family Photo*

CHAPTER 8

Our Mountain Town
Is Quarantined

O ctober 1887 found us settled in a new home — down in "the city," a change far from welcome to Brother and me, whose hearts had been left behind up at No. 7. We had for some time awaited the opportunity to move into the Joe Davis house, which, though conveniently located halfway between the schoolhouse and business center, was in unsanitary proximity to a slaughterhouse. Its superior convenience did not compensate for our loss of freedom to roam at large over the mountainside.

Trees and shrubbery and flowers were on the hill above our home, but they were not our familiar friends of the higher slopes. Most of the trees were of the same species but of somewhat smaller growth. They were, however, easier to climb, and the following summer when a circus came to town, Brother was inspired to imitate the acrobats; he became entangled between a rope and a tree branch. According to the man who rescued him, "He had been trying to hang himself," but this Brother always stoutly denied.

The quartz mill at the No. 9 tunnel was located near the road into Sierra City and next to Busch's Flat and the new mine office. *Thomas Family Photo*

Calamity sounded when, in the first week of October, the whistle blew at No. 9 after everyone had retired, summoning every miner to duty. The old Hitchcock mill was burning[1] at No. 7, and it was a total loss, being without insurance.

The Buttes Mine's new office, mill and chlorination works had all been wired for electricity, and Sept. 3, 1887, would long be remembered in Sierra City as the day the current was turned on. It was perhaps the high point of the great mine's improvements, for all was not well there. By the end of June, the *Mountain Messenger* had reported completion of the upraise between No. 8 and No. 9 tunnels, with No. 9 driven in 8,000 feet "at a total cost of between $150,000 and $200,000," the article ending with the ominous note, "and all without profit to the company."[2] And all without finding the faulting vein.

Attending school was a new experience. Brother was in the primary room under kind Miss White while I was under the redoubtable Mr. Wickson, who instructed all the other grades, and of whose reputation as a man of hasty temper I was in happy ignorance. School having been in session since Aug. 3, I was experimentally assigned to the lowest class and achieved my first day there without mishap. It was to be my only day under that stern disciplinarian, for on that very afternoon I fell ill of the measles, which had plagued the town for the two preceding months.[3]

Mother had barely time to congratulate herself on having nursed Brother and me through our attack of measles before I contracted a more serious disease. Typhoid fever had become prevalent in this mountain town, but, by "God's mercy," Mother said, I was the only one stricken in our family. There were three long anxious weeks, when Mother was my only nurse, but I survived, and (perhaps this was the greater marvel) my wonderful Mother survived as well.

As my strength slowly returned, and I was able to help Mother by running short errands to Busch's Store nearby, I heard the pitying comments of street loungers along my way and was made conscious of the loss of my long hair, which was especially deplored.

But before this unhappy year had come to an end, our town was to experience an epidemic worse even than typhoid. With no hospital and in a county that had no Board of Health, a case of smallpox developed in Mitchell's

Sierra City school in 1888. Mabel could be in the fourth row in front of the girl with the wide straw hat.

Hotel, a favorite resort of the miners. It had been brought from San Francisco by a man who, while claiming to be recovering from (the less serious) chickenpox, had circulated freely about, going as far as Sierra Valley.

An appeal for funds to meet this crisis was refused by the supervisors at Downieville on the grounds that they lacked any such authority under state law. Gripped by panic, Downieville set up a quarantine against Sierra City, refusing to allow its mail to be carried nearer than six miles, and even turning back the city's winter beef supply because it had been driven through the stricken town. No. 7 had declared

Courtesy of the Sierra County Historical Society

its own quarantine against the city below, and citizens of Loganville, all 13 in number, forbade all communication with its neighbor above.

On Dec. 16, a group of citizens gathered in Masonic Hall comprising William James, representing the Buttes Mine, our father, Stephen Thomas, representing the Masons, and a representative from each of the other secret orders of the town. Doctors Tully and Spedding were summoned, and pronounced the disease "smallpox in modified form, contagious."

The following measures were adopted:

1. Churches, schools, dance houses, and some saloons were ordered closed, and public gatherings forbidden.
2. A subscription was to be taken to defer initial expenses.
3. Of those present, seven were elected to serve as a Health Committee — O.L. Moore, R. Jenkins, W.M. James, J. Hayes, J.C. Hopper, J.E. Wickson, and I. Perry. Mr. Hopper, who was one of Superintendent Preston's office force, was made secretary, and Dr. Spedding was appointed Health Officer.
4. Guards were to be placed to enforce the quarantine.
5. Vaccination was made compulsory.
6. Owners of dogs were to be ordered to keep them at home.
7. The man who had gone about the county scattering disease was to be jailed. (Two cases had been reported in Downieville and two in Sattley.)

8. A pest house was to be built in the woods outside the town and staffed by men who had had the disease.
9. The Health Committee was to meet every evening at 7:30.

The actions so promptly decided were as rigidly enforced. From the front windows of our little house above the street along which patients were conveyed to the new house in the woods, we children kept watch for the gruesome "Black Maria," as we named the smallpox sleigh.

It was a winter long to be remembered, one that seemed long in passing. Dr. Tully was our only caller as he made his rounds of professional visits, returning again and again to re-vaccinate Brother, on whom the virus seemed to refuse to take. Brother might perhaps be pardoned for rejoicing when the good doctor, after vaccinating some 220 persons, himself fell ill of the contagion.

A number of cases developed, but all were cared for, men in the pest house, women in the homes. There were but two deaths, and by the end of February the epidemic seemed at an end. Already a petition had been sent to the new Board of Health in Downieville asking that it order removal of the Sierra City slaughterhouses to a location outside the town.[4]

When the supervisors had drawn up a Contagious Disease Ordinance, dividing the county into five health districts, they levied a tax of $2 on each male between the ages of 21 and 60, and named our Health Committee of seven a Board of Health for Sierra City. The *Messenger*, on Dec. 31, reported between 20 and 30 cases in the town, and the *Sierra Tribune* on Jan. 13 reported 25 cases.

On Feb. 11, Sierra City's mail had been allowed to move,[5] and on March 17, with the discharge of the last patient from the pest house, the public school was re-opened. The Health Committee wound up its affairs on April 7 by billing the supervisors for $1,596.31, having raised by subscription an additional $1,291.52, total expenses, $2,888.33.[6]

Even before the indomitable committee had closed its accounts, the eager town had begun to show its joy over relief from quarantine. The Sierra Buttes Band led off on Feb. 24 with a social dance, ending with supper at Soracco's, and followed the next week with a concert and dance at Moore's Hall. Its rival Sierra City Band, not to be outdone, announced a grand ball and supper for the following Friday. The Colombo Restaurant was advertising fresh oysters every day, while Jimmie Hill's promised "ice cream today and tomorrow," a luxury usually reserved for the Fourth of July. Not so pleasant was the *Sierra Tribune's* news: "A calaboose is to be erected here," and "Bad boys chew tobacco and use bad language . . . Dance houses are patronized by youths of 15 years and up."[7]

News of the epidemic, reaching San Francisco and reported with picturesque exaggeration in that city's papers, may have inspired two bits of news covered in our own *Sierra Tribune*: "Mrs. Ettie Wood is arriving next week with millinery and hat trimmings" . . . and W.L. Thurston, Nevada City photographer, will arrive soon."[8]

June brought plans for making the coming Fourth of July the greatest celebration ever known in Sierra City. In the meantime there was the annual Sunday School picnic on June 14.[9] This event, always a general town holiday, would this year attract visitors from far and near, and every housewife had made extraordinary preparations. Such a baking of cakes and pies and such a roasting of meats for sandwiches as went on in every kitchen had seldom been known even in Sierra City, and prodigious numbers of oranges and lemons had been provided by the merchants for the liquid refreshments for the occasion.

When clouds veiled the sky on the day of the picnic, there was general dismay. Yes, it rained and rained hard! With luncheons all ready for packing and the Buttes Band in full uniform assembled for playing, something had to be done to save the day. With simplicity of genius, the problem was solved, for was not Adam Moore's hall empty and large enough to accommodate crowds, adults as well as children?

Somewhat muted, the band played, and games too were played, and luncheons were eaten, and all agreed that there was even more sociability than would have been possible on the wide spaces of an ordinary picnic ground.

Boys dressed as minutemen, probably for a July 4 celebration in the mid-1890s. Willard is the boy at the far left. *Thomas Family Photo*

CHAPTER 9

Our Patriotic Holidays

There were two days of each year when the outlying population of Sierra City could be expected to flock into town from all the surrounding territory.

On Memorial Day and on the Fourth of July, every soul who could ride, drive, or walk would be there. From every outlying canyon, mountain top, ravine or gulch the miners would come, all who had not arrived on the night before appearing before 9:30 a.m., when the grand parade would begin to form.

The two processions were as different as the two days. The Civil War was, in the 80s, too vividly remembered by too many to make Memorial Day other than a solemn occasion. Then the band played the "Battle Hymn of the Republic," and old soldiers from either side would mingle in the carriages. President Lincoln's Gettysburg Address would be read, and school children would recite such verses as Whittier's "Barbara Frietschie" or Francis Miles Finch's "The Blue and the Gray":

> By the flow of the inland river,
> Whence the fleets of iron have fled

Where the blades of the grave-grass quiver,
Asleep are the ranks of the dead:
Under the sod and the dew,
Waiting the judgment-day;
Under the one the Blue;
Under the other the Gray.

. . . No more shall the war-cry sever
Or the winding river be red;
They banish our anger forever
Who laurel the graves of our dead!
Under the sod and the dew,
Waiting the Judgment Day,
Love and tears for the Blue,
Tears and love for the Gray.

The orator of the day might be a clergyman, and if there were soldiers' graves in the cemetery, it was there the ceremony would end in prayer.

Our glorious Fourth began at dawn with ringing of bells and a noise we heard but once a year, made by blasts of powder on a blacksmith's anvil (substituting for the big guns lacking in our mountain seclusion). We children somehow managed to waken in time to hear the patriotic clamor ushering in this one of the two greatest days of our year.

If Christmas was our apogee, Independence Day ranked only slightly second in rejoicing, being in some ways more full of excitement. A nationwide festival, in which "liberty would be proclaimed throughout the land to all the inhabitants thereof," it was of vital interest to every man, woman or child. The *Messenger's* account in 1885 closely parallels that of Sierra City in the same paper. Here is its report of E Clampus Vitus' part in the day:[1]

> The parade of the Brothers of Balaam Lodge No. 107,304 started from the Temple at 8 p.m., led by the Noble Grand Humbug, riding the direct descendant of steed in sacred history. The Sierra City Brass Band followed in full regalia . . . . Then came the jewels of the Order, followed by 100 brethren in good standing. The multitude was addressed by D.F.A.K., (a popular young orator) and our ever eloquent Sister Eve, who (notwithstanding her advanced age) has fine powers of delivery. The band then played the Clampers' Ode.

For such festivity, great were the preparations made by housewives and merchants alike. For the ladies of the Methodist Church there was the special responsibility of providing (for a profit) the ice cream, which everyone expected to find on sale on this occasion. Several days before, boys would be sent to the top of the Buttes to procure the necessary ice and carry it down on mule back. The same boys would be set to turning the freezers, which the ladies filled with custards, heavily loaded with cream and flavored either with lemon or vanilla.

Sierra City seemed in 1888 to reach a climax of prosperity. It was also the year of its most memorable Fourth of July celebration, of which the *Messenger's* detailed description is here quoted:[2]

At an early hour the people were crowding the streets fully prepared to appropriately celebrate the National Jubilee. All the business houses and residences were seen proudly waving in the breeze the red, white, and blue. Visitors from Downieville and other adjacent towns continued to arrive, taxing the hotel-keepers to their utmost to accommodate their guests.

The procession was formed at 9:30 a.m. at the Odd Fellows Hall, led by the Sierra Buttes Band. First came the Goddess of Liberty, Miss Kitty Bigelow; then George and Martha Washington (Montford Crowell and Dollie Ferrari), and Miss California Gertrude Smith; followed by Eureka Fire Company; Native Sons of Downieville and Sierra City and Knights of Pythias. The procession was under the direction of F. Trebilcox, aided by Peter Seitz and Harry Gorham. (Also participating were :) President of the Day, Bert Schlesinger; Chaplain, James Nichols; reader of Declaration of Independence, Master Willie Copren; and Orator of the Day, Tirey L. Ford,

Portions of Mr. Ford's eloquent speech are here reproduced:

On this day, to us the most memorable of all the year . . . we forget our personal cares and grievances, and give way to our patriotic feelings. From Plymouth Rock, across New England's hills, spreading out into the broad basin of the

Mississippi, rolling across the western plains and climbing over the mountain barriers that divide a continent, there come to us the mingled shouts and songs of American freemen, and as this grand chorus, gathering volume in its western course, breaks in upon our golden state, a million throats with wild acclaim, send up their glad rejoicings, and the God of Nations looks benignly down upon a happy race of freemen.

Here, in this quiet corner of our favored land, we, too, with music, speech, and song come to pay our tribute to the American flag, and to honor the memory of those daring men, who with courage and fidelity unparalleled in history, defied the most powerful monarch of his times, and revolutionized the existing laws of civilization . . . We celebrate the valorous deeds of American heroes, who, casting aside all thoughts of favor or of fear, proclaimed to the world that all men are by nature free, and that all government should rest upon the consent of the governed . . . Traversing more than a century of time, we find ourselves in the midst of a revolution that was destined to change the current of political thought throughout the civilized world . . .

The first battle smoke that arose from Lexington carried into ethereal space all hope of reconciliation between colonist and crown, and as the curtain fell upon the last act of that bloody drama at Yorktown, imperial rule was forever banished from American soil. From the ashes of that revolution there came forth a new government such as the world had never seen. That government, founded on the immortal declaration of July 4, 1776, was reared aloft by hands 'that builded better than they know' . . .

As the first gun at Sumter put our nation on trial for its life, so from Appomattox went up a decree that 'we should not perish from the nations of the earth!' . . . My friends, we who have for a time become the tenants of this vast estate, are indeed fortunate among the peoples of earth. For us a continent was wrenched from despotic hands, consecrated with fraternal blood, and set upon the highest pinnacle of the nations of modern times. For us the blood of patriotic sires was spilled upon the battlefield, and the voice of eloquence rang out in our behalf. Political and religious liberty was stamped upon every foot of American soil . . .

Standing here amid the echoing canyons of Sierra's lofty hills, and looking across broad expanse of mountain, river and plain, to where the sunlight first kisses the shore of New England, we behold a land that has dazzled the historian and astonished a world.

The parade had wound up on Busch's Flat, where the oration, which was the leading feature of the day's program, was delivered from a speaker's stand. "It was said by those who heard it," commended the *Messenger*, "to be one of the ablest efforts ever listened to in Sierra County. The exercises of the afternoon consisted of the installation of the officers elected of Balaam Lodge No. 107,304, E Clampus

Vitus (ECV), conducted by the GPNGH, Judge Lemon of Moses Lodge, Sierra Valley, after which there were races by men, boys and young ladies, hotly contested; and a tight rope performance by Jack Crossman. In the evening the Clampers turned out in torch-light procession, which was appreciated by all those who saw them. Salutes were fired, and there was a display of fireworks. Grand orator, Frank Lee, Esq., ably delivered the annual oration of the ECV.

"The day's proceedings closed with an all-night dance on an open platform in the city park, the music being furnished by the Sierra City String Band. This is the largest gathering of people ever assembled at any time in Sierra City."

A tightrope walker performs for the Fourth of July in Sierra City. *Courtesy of the Sierra County Historical Society*

Sierra City after a heavy snow storm. *Courtesy of the Sierra County Historical Society*

CHAPTER 10

Our Alpine Winter

What had seemed to be for Sierra City in 1888 a year of climactic prosperity was not without portents of decline for the great mine on which much of that prosperity depended.

On Dec. 10, a loss was suffered in the death of Superintendent Preston. Although not a mining man, he had comprised an indispensable link with the owners of the mine, the Buttes Company in London, and his tactful cooperation with Mr. James, the mine manager, had contributed much to its success.

Mr. Preston was not replaced, and now full responsibility fell upon Mr. James, who had been spending much of his time examining mines offered for sale. His title of foreman was in February bestowed upon Father, who had been carrying on many of his supervisory duties. They became even heavier when the company finally decided to purchase the Uncle Sam Mine in Shasta County, requiring still more of Mr. James' attention.

A new omen in Buttes Mine history was the discharge of 40 men in March 1889, reducing the working force to 160. Meanwhile, the ill-fated No. 9 tunnel was daily driven farther into the mountain, still without striking that elusive missing vein, and, by August, the Buttes monthly cleanup had dropped to a low of $9,500, contrasting with Young America's $25,800.

New disaster struck when a campfire left burning at Loganville by Sierra Valley plum pickers spread up the mountain, burning timber owned by the company. It raged from Aug. 19 to 26, destroyed the Independence mill and shaft, and filled the mine tunnels with gas and smoke. All Buttes men had been called out to fight the fire, and, before it was extinguished, one miner, Mr. Hansen, had been burned to death.

As a result of this catastrophe, all upper workings of the mine below No. 3 were out of commission, and early in October a contingent of miners left to work in the company's new mine in Shasta County.[1] A number of families also left town, and by the end of the month, only 30 men were employed.[2] The Buttes cleanup for November was $8,500 and the Sierra Buttes Band gave its last concert in Buttes Park on Aug. 25, many of its members being about to leave for Butte, Montana.

❧

There had been many heavy winters since 1852, when Sierra City's first settlement had been crushed by the weight of snow on its neglected roofs, but later residents had profited by the lesson, keeping their houses clear of this threat. Against the menace of avalanches, however, there could be no provision other than avoidance of building in ravines, but the town's most severe winters had passed without snow slides, and this precaution had too often been neglected.

In April, 1880, several snow slides in Reis Ravine had wrecked five arrastras and carried away the covering of the No. 7 tunnel. In 1882, as early as February, a seven-week storm had kept 100 of the Buttes miners out of work because of avalanches. Five years later, on Feb. 12, a man was killed by a slide at Keystone Mine near the top of the ridge across the river from Loganville. A week later, what was said to be the heaviest storm since 1850 had brought 3 ½ feet of snow to Downieville, with correspondingly greater depths at all higher levels. No stage from below could reach the town for two weeks, and what mail and express did arrive were carried by way of the river.

Even in the severe winter of 1887, no building in Sierra City had been swept away by a snow slide and records kept since 1850 showed heaviest storms coming not earlier than January or February, and sometimes as late as March or April.

The winter of 1889-90, however, was exceptional. At Sierra City, snow began to fall early in December. The *Sierra County Tribune* reported on Dec. 13, "Two feet of the beautiful in Sierra City," and on Dec. 20, "Still snowing — 5 feet in town." No danger was anticipated, and Christmas and New Year's Day were observed much as usual, although already there was some shortage of provisions in the stores.

Our family had moved from Joe Davis' house to one of Mr. Bigelow's new houses near the Pianezzi Ranch at the lower end of town. Although it was but a short distance from our front door to the front gate, I recall that Father, setting out to work one morning, was, after a full hour of struggle to reach the front gate, forced to turn back to the house, so great was the force of the wind.

Jan. 3, 1890, was a clear day, but in Sierra City the snow had attained a depth of 8 feet, and one could but wonder how deep it might be at the Buttes summit. That afternoon a party of skiers taking advantage of the beautiful day passed by our house, which faced a spur of the mountain ascending across the street. School was still in vacation, and we children were watching the sport, when Tom James came with news from his father — dire news of an avalanche that only minutes before had destroyed the three houses in closest proximity to our schoolhouse. All available men had been mustered there to begin the task of excavation.

Men work to dig out after an avalanche. *Courtesy of the Sierra County Historical Society*

The following account was written of the scene of disaster on Friday afternoon, Jan. 3:[3]

About 3 p.m. news was received that a snow slide coming from the direction of the Butte Saddle Mine[4] had completely buried the houses of I.T. Mooney, Mrs. Rich, and others in that section of town. The house of Mrs. Rich, in the center of the advancing slide and receiving the main force of the shock, was shivered to pieces and literally blotted out. Pieces of wood, boards, shingles, furniture, kitchen utensils, bird cages, dishes, with trunks and clothing, all were carried along in a mass for some distance. The house of I.T. Mooney was similarly destroyed, and that of Mrs. Lewis so wrecked as to be unfit for habitation.

Below on Busch's Flat, the main part of the Catholic Church was completely demolished, only the belfry being left standing. The houses of Mrs. Haitz and Mrs. Noblet just escaped — the snow broke in doors and windows and covered the sides from 15 to 30 feet deep. The porch of Mrs. Buscombe's house was ripped off, turned 3/4 around, and carried into the road.

Many people were buried in drifts. The body of Miss Amelia Ryan was brought out, and, except for slight discoloration, looked perfectly natural, a peaceful and resigned expression on her fair young face. Miss Etta Rich was found nearby, also dead; and after a long search the bodies of Mrs. Rich and her little boy were found. No trace (has been found) as yet of Mrs. Mooney or of the Misses Ethel Langton and Hattie Rich. (At this point, much of Mooney's house was found to be on fire, which could not be put out for some hours.)

After many unsuccessful attempts, Mr. Mooney and daughter were found by Captain James, Mr. J.H. Henderson and Mr. Grant . . . They were placed on improvised biers and carried to Masonic Hall. The Native Daughters of the Golden West took charge, and Mrs. Rich and family were taken to Good Templars' Hall.

By midnight, the search was given up for the night, leaving a guard. About 5 a.m. Saturday the fire bell rang — the ruins were again in flames, but were soon extinguished. Hattie Rich was found early Saturday morning. If the entire mass of snow had come down and swept everything into the river, many more would have been killed. Residents of Busch's Flat and of eastern and northern parts of town left their homes, fearing more slides.

Still to record is the miraculous escape of the Lewis family.

Mrs. Lewis somehow burrowed through the snow and escaped unhurt under the windows, freeing her children also. Two children of Mrs. Noblet on the flat below had also been buried by snow, and, by the time the second one was rescued, he was near to suffocation.

The little town, which had weathered so many winter storms, was now in the grip of fear. Who could feel safe?

RESIDENCE OF I.T. MOONEY,
SIERRA CITY, SIERRA CO., CAL.

The home of I.T. Mooney in Sierra City, probably before
the tragic avalanche of January 1890. *Courtesy of the Sierra
County Historical Society*

Those in the neighborhood of the slide were the first to
move, but Butte Street was also felt to be in grave danger, as
were many locations on Main Street. Buttes Ravine, with all
its arrastras, was under general suspicion as the most likely
site of the next avalanche.

It came two weeks later. Mr. James, whose house was
situated on a slope not far above the ravine, rose from a sick
bed to warn his neighbors to move out. Many had sought
safety in the depths of No. 9 tunnel, and the cross tunnel
leading from the ore house to No. 9 mill was now fitted
up as a refuge. When the dreaded avalanche did materialize

on Jan. 17, no life was lost, "although the snow must have reached a depth of 50 feet just below the bridge, coming up the sides of the ravine as high as Mr. James' house, but it ran on out, assuming the shape of the ravine." The bridge having been carried away, steps were cut in the snow, enabling people to go down into and out of the ravine.

The county bridge was also a total loss, and the house of Sam Oren was destroyed, as were the Buttes Mine dump house just above the bridge, its blacksmith shop just east of the bridge and a number of arrastras in the flat near the river. Some doubt was expressed as to whether the slide had demolished the No. 7 mill up above.

It had, indeed, been totally destroyed, and, higher up on the mountain, a portion of the flume had been swept away, but Mr. James, in his weakened state, was persuaded not to go up there. Officers of the Buttes Company now put all company stores at the disposal of any persons in need.

Still the unprecedented storm continued. On Jan. 18, the *Mountain Messenger* recorded an extraordinary depth of snow, 25 feet at Gold Lake, 20 feet at Mountain House and at Forest City, and 10 feet at Sierra City. A week later, a slide below the Marguerite Mine carried away the Lindstrom place, killing a mother and son.

By Jan. 31, Sierra City, with 12 feet of snow, had been visited by an epidemic of "la Grippe," and a third avalanche had carried away the homes of R. Jenkins, J. Fletcher, and Mrs. Cain, all of whom had fortunately moved out.[5] There was also the problem of a growing scarcity of provisions in the stores. "Butter was $1 per roll, eggs 75 cents a dozen, and flour $4 the hundred pound. Potatoes could not be purchased, and beef was something people had forgotten about."[6]

The hardships of life in the beleaguered town were aggravated by the lack of communication with the outside world. What scanty mail arrived had been carried on snowshoes by way of the river, and newspapers could not be delivered at all. The train from Colfax to Nevada City began to run on Feb. 7, after being blocked by snow for 19 days.[7] The telegraph to Sierra City was reported down on Feb. 22, and the stage from Nevada City was "unable to reach within 3 miles of the Mountain House."[8]

On that date, Downieville had 8 feet of snow and Nevada City 49 inches. On the Sierra City level it did not exceed a height of 15 feet except in ravines, where repeated snow slides accumulated so great a depth of snow that it formed great bridges across the river, which remained throughout the succeeding summer. Everywhere men had been kept employed shoveling snow from roofs.

Not until March was it deemed safe to open the schoolhouse which had so narrowly escaped destruction on Jan. 3. It is to be feared that my brother and I enjoyed the prolonged holiday far more than did our patient parents, but, fortunately, we were diligent readers of books borrowed from the new school library, which, in the preceding year, had been purchased under Mr. Albee. Oddly, I remember best my reading of Edward Bellamy's *Looking Backward, 2000-1887*, published in 1888. (Bellamy's description of a social utopia is said to have caused a sensation nearly as great as did Henry George's *Progress and Poverty* in 1879)

The Buttes Mine was still employing 11 men, and Charley James remained in residence at No. 7, where the big boarding house, the store, and a number of houses and cabins had withstood all the winter storms. Services of Dr. Tully, the mine physician were retained until April.

Although Mr. James was now obliged to give most of his attention to the Shasta County mine, his family did not leave their Sierra City home until Sept. 19 and they left Charley still on watch at No. 7.

On Aug. 1, President Tendron, accompanied by Mr. Johns, came over to visit from London. Mr. James arrived from Shasta County, and it was then decided that Father would not join Mr. James at the Uncle Sam Mine, but would re-open the Buttes Mine as soon as the No. 7 mill could be rebuilt. In the meantime, Father would take a course in surveying at the School of Mines in San Francisco, leaving his family in Grass Valley, where we remained until the end of November, when, after disposing of our furniture we returned to Sierra City, to occupy the Buttes Mine office.

Our arrival was the signal for the departure of Mr. Briggs, the office bookkeeper, and for the release of faithful Charley James from his long tour of duty at No. 7. Responsibility for all the Buttes Mine properties now rested upon Father. He lost no time in ordering lumber for a new mill at No. 7 and in setting men to repair the damage to the flume resulting from the hard winter.

The *Sierra County Tribune* listed other mines expected to be in operation in the spring of 1891: Young America, 160 men; Independence, Colombo Mountain, 150 men; Cleveland, 40 men; Marguerite, 60 men; Salinas and Mercer, 30 men; Chips, 25 men; California, 10 men; Northern

Belle, 10 men; Butte Saddle, 25 men; Mountain Ledge, Crowell Co., 20 men.

State Resources announced publication of a number reports on Sierra County in October 1890, and the "10th Report of the State Mineralogist, 1889/90" pronounced the Sierra City district to be "the richest in the county — veins of quartz and gravel course through it at all angles."

A Cornish housewife prepares pasties. Cover of a 1929 recipe book published by the Women's Institute of Cornwall

CHAPTER 11

Jack Tremain Comes Home

Busch's Flat in the 80s was the setting for some of Sierra City's great occasions. Here we celebrated the Queen's Jubilee in fittingly grand style, and here a traveling circus found room to spread its tents. In the lower portion, sloping down to the river, some of we children enjoyed a sheltered place to play baseball and other favorite games.

Mrs. Tremain's house was close by, across a grassy meadow, traversed by a little stream, in which she cooled her milk and butter. We always called it *Mrs.* Tremain's house, as her husband was away most of the time at a mine he was working up near Round Lake.

The oldest of her three sons was our playmate, John Jr., who would have chosen to be called Jack like his father, had his mother not insisted upon what he considered the babyish Johnny. Craving other society than that of his two young brothers, over whom his mother expected him to keep vigilant watch, he often urged us to accompany him on his way home, and we sometimes ventured timidly as far as Mrs. Tremain's back door, where we could look in on the kitchen's spotless floor and walls, its gleaming pots and pans, and a cook stove so diligently blacked and burnished that its iron surfaces could have reflected our faces.

Mrs. Tremain was considered a notable housekeeper even in Sierra City where it was generally believed that her tables and her kitchen floor were scrubbed, and her kitchen stove newly polished, not merely every Friday, but every day of the week (Sundays, of course, excepted). No less enticing than the sights were the odors that wafted our way as we stood just outside her door. It might be the spicy aroma of baking saffron buns or the even more tantalizing fragrances of golden brown pasties freshly drawn from the oven. Although we never ventured to set foot on that clean, clean, floor, Mrs. Tremain always greeted us kindly, and no

An advertisement for stove blacking from the 1895 Chatterbox

child departed without the gift of a cookie, a doughnut, or a piece of ginger cake.

Mrs. Tremain's house was fairly typical of many houses of that period built for rental to miners with families. Four steps led up from a small entrance yard to the front door, flanked on either side by a window and opening into a narrow passage, which extended back to the kitchen and separated the two other rooms, on the right a bedroom, on the left a parlor, usually known as the "front room." Not all miners' front rooms were quite as luxuriously furnished as this one with its Brussels carpet, lace curtains, and even several pieces of upholstered furniture, covered with a satin brocade.

While, to a critical eye, the orange flowers of the paper might appear somewhat to clash with the red ground and bright pink roses of the carpet, it did not diminish Mrs. Tremain's satisfaction in her possession of a parlor, appropriately furnished and adorned with a number of pieces of her own handiwork, including a mantel lambrequin of macramé work, several cushions covered with fine net, darned in intricate patterns, and on the wall a fan-shaped patchwork of varicolored silks, joined together by what was known as crazy stitch. Although such a room was far too fine for daily use, Mrs. Tremain found an enjoyment in its daily dusting and weekly "turning out" which was only slightly diminished by her recollection of a certain autumn morning when she had found a rattlesnake coiled under one of the lace curtains.

The kitchen, extending across the rear of the house and occupying more than half its total floor space, was the family living room, where meals were eaten as well as cooked, and where all could sit and take their ease. There was a comfortable rocking chair for Mother and a somewhat larger one for Father in his rare leisure days at home. On one side a ladder-like stairway gave access to a loft, in which the three boys slept at night. Their mother found it most convenient, for on no account would she permit them to enter the front portion of the house without first removing their shoes.

Early on Monday mornings, a wash boiler was mounted on the stove and three wash tubs were fetched in from the woodshed, thus transforming the kitchen into a laundry, where all the weekly washing was performed. On Saturday evenings it underwent a similar change, when it was made to serve as the family bathroom.

This kitchen possessed two conveniences not always found in mountain dwellings of that day. There was a small sink with running water, and a hot water boiler stood beside the wood range. The house unfortunately lacked a summer kitchen into which the range could be removed at the beginning of summer, to remain until autumn would bring cooler days. Several windows provided ventilation, however, and these were equipped with the uncommon luxury of screens.

Since there was no bakery in Sierra City, all bread, cakes, and pastry, were homemade. In every well-ordered kitchen Saturday was one of the two weekly baking days, and on a certain warm Saturday in August, could we have looked in on Mrs. Tremain's kitchen we should have found her risen early, the fire already kindled and the oven heating, in preparation for an expected guest.

On this day, her husband was returning after three months absence at the mine. To secure the requisite degree of heat for her varied program of baking and cooking would tax even her skill in managing the wood-burning range.

For the necessary supply of wood, split into several different sizes, she would require the assistance of her two oldest boys. The sponge for her bread (made from her own potato yeast) she had set the night before, wrapping it warmly that it might increase by morning to the right bulk for mixing.

Modern cookbooks still offer directions for yeast breads, but we are fortunately able to follow every step of the method used by Mrs. Tremain in a handbook used by brides of the 80s, Marion Harland's *Common Sense in the Household*. Before breakfast, she must add the due amount of flour, remembering Marion's injunction to devote at least 20 minutes to a "brisk and long kneading."

"Half an hour is better," continued her mentor, "in this kind of useful gymnastics. It is grand exercise for arms and chest."

The dough must again be covered and left in a warm place to rise "for four or five hours." When it should have "at least trebled, "would be the time for another "10 to 15 minutes kneading," after which it would be formed into loaves and placed in well-greased pans for still another (and final) rising. At the end of another hour, the bread should be ready to be popped into the oven, from which, "after a long, slow baking," it might be expected to emerge in the shape of seven pale brown, crusty loaves, good to look at, good to smell, and best of all to taste.

But for Mrs. Tremain, this happy moment was still several hours away, and the "sponge" she had set for saffron cake was demanding her attention, when she saw that her stock of wood was sadly diminished. No boys responded to her call, nor were they in sight when she ran outside to look for them.

"John-nee," she called, "John-nee! Where are you?"

Snatching an armful of wood, she returned to the kitchen to replenish the fire, muttering threats the while against that good-for-nothing son of hers. "I'll take a stick to 'en, I will that! To run away with little brothers, and me with all this on my hands!"

"Gee, Ma!" cried an already repentant Johnny appearing at the door. "I was only running up to the store for one little minute to see if Pa had come."

"A fine excuse when you well know your Pa never do come this early," she retorted. "But he'll be here before I have his pasties done, with the fire dying down and you leaving the wood box empty. Get to work now before I take a stick to 'ee!"

Armfuls of fuel were hurried in by all three boys, and their mother was mollified by the sound of Johnny's axe splitting larger pieces to the thinness needed for the degree of heat suited to each of the oven's varied tasks.

"Move quick now, Johnny," she urged, "do 'ee go for the meat right away, and leave your brothers to mind the wood for me while you're gone. Listen! Don't forget to tell Mr. Seitz you want that good steak for the pasties and the roast for tomorrow's dinner I showed him yesterday. And mind 'ee — no dilly dallying' along the way! I want 'ee back inside of 10 minutes, do 'ee hear?

"Yes, Ma," shouted Johnny, already bounding up the trail to Main Street and Mr. Seitz's butcher shop.

First the saffron cake, then the bread, emerged from the oven in triumphantly final state, their places being immediately filled by the pasties and blackberry pie. Since no Cornishman could consider this complete without a topping of his favorite Cornish cream[1], Mrs. Tremain had not forgotten to obtain this delicacy from a neighbor who kept a cow.

The boys had made several dashes to and from the express office in Busch's Store, where their father would pause to deposit his bullion before making his way down to the house. A fragrance from the oven indicated that the pasties were nearly done, and Mrs. Tremain had laid the cloth for the homecoming meal, when warning shouts from her sons sent her hurrying to the front door just in time to be the first sight to meet her husband's eye as he came down the path with little Tommy on his back, and a son on either side.

Her greeting?

"Mind 'ee Tremain! Don't 'ee dirty up my clean front steps! Take the boys around to the back door!"

Cornish Pasties

2 servings

Note: Ideally the crust should be shortened with beef suet, finely chopped, but Mabel Thomas used a pie crust mix in her later years.

Use short-crust pastry (American pie crust mix, each package making two large pasties) or make four pie crusts.

1 pound round steak, cut into small cubes
1 cup raw potatoes, diced
1¼ cup onion, chopped
salt
pepper
finely chopped celery or parsley
2½ tablespoons butter
8 tablespoons cream (optional)

Mix together everything but the butter and cream. Dot with butter.

Roll each crust out on lightly floured board to circle the size of a dinner plate (about 10 inches) and ¼ inch thick.

Place on one-half of the pastry circle one-quarter of the mixture.

Wet the edges of filled half of each circle. Fold the plain half over the filled half, pinching the edges together firmly with fingers. Prick the top, to allow escape of steam. Brush over with beaten egg or milk. Bake on sheet for approximately 1 hour, 45 minutes, in 325 degree oven. Remove from oven and make small incision in each and pour in two tablespoons of cream (optional). Bake for 15 more minutes.

Postscript

Editor's note: After looking through all the notes Mabel left behind, I found that she had ideas for perhaps 10 more chapters that she never accomplished. Amidst her notes was, however, a half-page of typed writing she never included in the previous chapters. A nostalgic tribute to the Cornish she once knew, it seems a fitting end to her memoir:

Letters from 'ome

However sincere the new citizens might be in renouncing allegiance to the British crown, there were still remaining many ties of memory and affection to bind them to their native country. Most, like my father, had left behind them parents, sisters and other relatives, some of them wholly or partly dependent upon them for support. Trips back to visit the old home were common among the men. I knew one woman whose husband was urged by her physician to return her to Cornwall for a time to cure a serious case of homesickness. This miner actually did so, though it meant being without wife and young children for more than a year.

Letters from 'ome is the name the Cornish in America have given their delicious pasties, which, I am persuaded, can be made to perfection only by Cornish hands. With help from my father, mother and I strove to acquire the art. (I still make them, knowing my product will probably never quite equal those made by such notable housewives and excellent cooks as I knew in the women from Cornwall.)

Other folkways and distinctive foods are cherished by descendants of the Cornish emigrants, the best known being their yuletide customs. After many, many years, I still can visualize in the old town hall of Sierra City one of the Christmas gatherings to which everyone came, bringing their children. I remember Dr. Iglick as he recited from *Pickwick Papers*, but yet more clearly I seem to hear the exquisite voice of our mountain songbird, little Polly Uren singing "Far Away," surely the saddest of all Christmas songs:

"Where is now the merry party I
remember long ago
Laughing round the Christmas fire, brightened
by its ruddy glow?
Or in summer's balmy evening in the
field upon the hay?
They are all dispersed and wandered, far
away, far away."

Afterword

While her father labored to make the Sierra Buttes Mine pay after reopening it in the spring of 1891, Mabel Thomas grew to maturity in the shadow of the Buttes.

Her intellectual precociousness bore fruit in 1893, when, at age 15, she won a trip with 20 other California students to the World's Fair in Chicago, sponsored by the *San Francisco Examiner* newspaper.

The *Examiner* naturally gave intensive coverage to this competition, devoting one entire article to the fact that Mabel and two other young women from remote areas presented themselves exceptionally well despite never having seen a fire engine, piped-in water, street cars, gas, electric bells or elevators. Indeed, Mabel took a written examination in seven subjects and received 631½ points of a possible 700, beating other students competing in her senatorial district (Plumas, Nevada, Butte, Sierra and Tehama counties) and finishing higher than three of the five San Francisco winners.

The *Examiner* referred to Mabel "as one of the brightest in the whole party," while stating "the mountains and forests of America do not stultify the intellect; they stimulate it." Perhaps it was the reporters that were naïve, not realizing how much magazines and books served to educate and inform people outside of cities.[1]

All of California celebrated the 21 students who passed rigorous exams in their districts, according to the *San Francisco Examiner*, and were awarded a place on a special train for the Chicago World's Fair in June 1893. Mabel is in the middle row, second from the right. *Thomas Family Photo*

The 21 young Californians became celebrities across the state, were showered with presents as they left on a special train called the Santa Ysabel while their days at the fair were reported at length. During a cruise on the lagoon at the center of the fair's splendid white buildings and golden statues, Mabel pops up in a reporter's story: "Little Mabel Thomas of Sierra drew a long breath. 'This,' she said, 'is the White City I have dreamed of'."

For Mabel's father, however, the years were less successful: In the 1896 report of the State Mineralogist, the Sierra Buttes Mine is described as "worked out," with Stephen Thomas as superintendent and 15 men at work.

By 1897, the Thomases saw the end of their Sierra City sojourn and moved "below" for good to Oakland east of Lake Merritt, in the same neighborhood that Jack London had lived with his mother, and where Gertrude Stein spent her childhood.

In 1898, Stephen took off on his last adventure, up to Alaska which was a disaster for many, including him. He never got a chance to apply his mining acumen along the Klondike — where some 30,000 were marching in with a year's provisions on their backs as required by the Canadian government — because his party left late, was blocked by ice on the river and he was stranded in the bitter cold.

In his diary, he wrote on March 31, 1899, his 50th birthday, "Oh, what years of toil they have been and now with a

Stephen Thomas, first row, second from left, continued to invest in and work various mines after leaving Sierra City for Oakland. Here he sits with the crew of the Central Eureka Mine in Sutter Creek, Amador County, that he likely owned with his older brother, William. *Thomas Family Photo*

body almost worn out, I am in ice-enclosed Alaska, looking for a fortune, but it seems further away than ever. All hope of success in this venture is abandoned by me."

As a lifelong inhabitant of dark, damp spaces, he had developed silicosis, a lung condition caused by the repeated inhalation of quartz dust, and the trip north severely weakened him. He returned with pneumonia, which he managed to survive, but died five years later after trying several other unsuccessful mining ventures in Calaveras and Amador counties.

In the meantime Mabel attended San Jose Teachers College and the University of California at Berkeley, graduating in 1901. After a brief stint as a school teacher in Crescent City, she returned to Oakland.

She joined the Oakland Public Library as a substitute librarian in 1905 and then helped her mother plan and direct the building of a large two-story home on 7th Avenue. The family was struck by tragedy when, on a rainy night before Christmas 1906, Mabel's youngest brother Arthur, who had just turned 20 and was an aspiring newspaper reporter, returned home from rehearsal for a local theatrical production and was electrocuted in the bathroom.

After a year of grieving, Mabel returned to the library as a regular librarian and spent 40 years working in the Oakland library, where she rose to Chief Reference Librarian.

She served as assistant for three male city librarians and acted in their stead when they were absent. She may have been reticent about self-promotion, but there was no doubt in the minds of anyone who knew her that she was capable of the handling the job of City Librarian. According to our family, the prejudices of the time prevented it.

Instead, she worked tirelessly to improve the library's reference service. She gloried in serving the public's need for information. Decades before Google, she left no stone unturned in digging up the answers to all manner of questions posed to her staff. In a 1929 interview with the *Oakland Tribune*, she said she loved the "stimulus of cracking the hard ones."[2]

Mabel encouraged her staff and stood by them. "She always had a smile, a joke, a quiet word of praise or advice to revive flagging spirits and help over rough spots," her friend and colleague Ethel Blumann wrote about her. "Many who later went into various fields of library work received from her their first glimpse of how creative a profession librarianship could be."[3]

Ethel assisted Mabel in editing a bibliography on California local history and together they guided a 1938 Works Progress Administration history of Oakland. Mabel also began in the 1920s to collect books, periodicals, clippings and indexes on California history that formed the basis for the library's California room, now the popular Oakland History Room.

In contrast to her very modern devotion to career and library work, she held to Edwardian customs for the rest of her life. She lived with her mother until her death in 1923. She never married, but had close women friends, including one who was her companion and roommate for many years.

An older cousin remembers going to visit her on Sunday and playing on a sofa swing in her wisteria-covered backyard as the roommate, a library colleague named Lucie Nye, prepared and served tea and cakes. Mabel decamped every summer to the elegant Tahoe Tavern on the shores of Lake

Tahoe; her arrival there listed in the social pages of the San Francisco papers.

Mabel's brother Willard married Lillian Laymance from Healdsburg and raised four children in the family home on 7th Avenue. Their children, including my father who was also called Willard, all raised their children (including me) in Oakland where Aunt Mabel kept an interested and indulgent eye on everyone. To the younger generation, she encapsulated old-fashioned traits of stern judgment and rectitude along with personal warmth.

Strangely enough, despite her work on this memoir Mabel returned to Sierra City rarely. She never drove a car and had to rely on others for transport. Instead, her brother Willard returned over the years with his family. He could always prod the driver to take on the rocky roads into the Buttes to look for the road to the No. 7 mine, promising the vistas were worth it.

Mabel and Willard began working on the memoir together sometime in the 1950s after Mabel's retirement from the library and Mabel continued it after Willard's death in 1958. Mabel was 87 when she died in April 1965.

— Laura Thomas

Later Years

Mabel Thomas, far left, at a 1957 family gathering in Oakland with the children, spouses and grandchildren of her brother Willard, back row, second man from left. Her great-niece, Laura, is seated in the front.

Mabel at the top of Glacier Point in Yosemite with her great-niece Pamela Quigley in 1958

Mabel and Willard Thomas on a visit to Grass Valley in the 1950s

At family gatherings, Mabel, right, often reminisced with Muriel Richards Quigley, her niece's mother-in-law. Mrs. Quigley was a survivor of the 1906 San Francisco earthquake and fire. Her father, Clayton French Richards, was a wholesale druggist and a founder of the Bohemian Club.

The Sierra Buttes Mine

F ew details of the Sierra Buttes Mine's early history have been preserved, but it is known to have been discovered in 1850 as an aftermath of the Stoddard Party's Gold Lake rush. Among the hundreds of adventurers who followed Stoddard, there was at least one experienced prospector, a Mexican named Manuel Gutierrez, who broke away from the disappointed company to explore the surrounding country. He chose to return by way of the Sierra Buttes Mountain, and, not far below its summit he located not only the mine to which the mountain gave its name, but the Independence Mine as well.

The outcroppings were bold and very rich, showing free gold. The soil and debris below the Sierra Buttes vein paid from $5 to $8 to the pan. The news soon reached Downieville, which for a time was depopulated. Merchants and miners, lawyers, washerwomen and doctors — on horse and foot — all started for the new El Dorado. The whole country was staked off, not even excepting the Buttes mountain to its crest, and a city (Sierra

City) was projected, now (in 1866) consisting of half a dozen houses.

The first discoverers and first locators of the lode, however, were the only ones who persevered to development. They leased the property to Messrs. Woods and Illingsworth, who, with Mexican labor, opened the mine and worked the ore by arrastras until 1856, in the meantime acquiring possession of the entire property.[1]

We are fortunate in possessing, in J.D. Borthwick's *Three Years in California,* a description of the mine in this first Mexican period.[2] Not a miner, but a traveler and a keen observer of the California scene, Borthwick landed in San Francisco in 1851, reaching Downieville in July of that year, shortly after the hanging of Juanita. He continued up the canyon of what was then known as the south fork of the North Fork of the Yuba River, to the foot of the Sierra Buttes Mountain.

"One of the highest mountains in the mines," he wrote, "thirty miles above Downieville (an exaggeration, but there was no road, and the trail was exceedingly rough.) He climbed the Buttes "from a cabin about 8 miles from the summit," halfway up coming in sight of a "quartz-grinding establishment in a very steep place where a small stream of water came dashing over the rocks. In the face of the hill a step had been cut out, on which a cabin was built, and immediately below were two 'rasters' in full operation." He describes a tramway used to bring the quartz from the vein several hundred yards above. The loaded car was supposed to bring up the empty one; but the railway was so steep that it looked as if a car once started would never stop until it reached the river, two or three miles below.

A wind came up in the night and so great was its force that Borthwick remained for two days a prisoner in the cabin. "Heavy gusts, coming down the chimney, filled the cabin with smoke, ashes, and burning wood" . . . and when he resumed his upward way, . . . grizzly bears infested the trail up the mountain." Climbing "with enormous difficulty the teeth of the saw," he exclaims on the vastness and beauty of the view — "Mt. Diablo 200 miles away!"

Wood and Illingsworth made the mistake in 1857 of supposing that they had worked their property to the point of exhaustion and offered for sale what they thought a worked-out mine.

It was purchased by the Reis brothers of San Francisco: Christian, Gustavus, Ferdinand, and Julius C. Reis.

According to a history of San Francisco published in 1892, they came across the plains to California in 1849, mining without a lot of success in Mariposa and Calaveras counties.[3] Going to Marysville, they engaged in freighting to the camps on the Yuba and Feather rivers and then started a store, a real estate and banking business in gold dust, at Downieville before ending up in San Francisco.[4]

After 13 years the Reis brothers sold the mine to English investors.

"A controlling interest in the Reis mine at Sierra City has been sold to an English company at a price asked on $750,000 as the aggregate value of the property."[5] They appear to have made the purchase on the recommendation of a San Francisco agent, Messrs. Cross and Company, based on the reports of two mining engineers. Henry Janin's account is here reproduced in full, since it gives descriptive details which seem nowhere else to be found.[6]

> The Sierra Buttes mine is approached by a mule trail, connecting with Downieville, 13 miles east of it. The Henness Pass wagon road, which connects with the Southern Pacific railroad at Emigrant Gap, passes within six miles of these mines. It is under contemplation to connect the mines with this road by a short road some six miles long, the estimated cost of which is $5,000. (Talked of for years, it was never done) . . . At present heavy pieces of machinery are transported to the ridge above the mines by ox teams, and thence lowered to the mines by block and tackle. These mines are among the earliest worked in California, dating back to 1851, when the quartz was crushed in arrastras. The property comprises three veins — the Rose, the Cliff, and the Ariel. They are enclosed in a country rock of hard metamorphic slate. They have a general east and west direction, with a dip to the north of from 30 to 40 degrees. The ledges are large, and have been proved over a great length; whenever exposed, the walls are found to be well defined: these and other general features of these ledges combine to assure great permanency in depth. Near the center of the hill on which the veins occur, the three veins converge and concentrate, going west, and becoming one...
> The workings of these three ledges are connected by crosscuts from the main working tunnels

which are driven in on the Ariel ledge. The ledges are variable in dimensions. Where the three veins converge, the quartz at times is more than 50 feet thick, while the veins before junction vary from 8 to 20 feet. The pay-ore, or productive zone of the ledges, varies also from 2 to 15 feet, and is found sometimes on the foot-wall, sometimes on the hanging wall, and often when the vein is large, in the middle, with barren quartz on either side. The Rose ledge is absorbed below the third level by the Ariel, but large reserves of good ore remain in it above that line . . . . The Ariel is the main ledge and the most valuable, both by reason of the value of its reserve, and on account of its promise for the future.

The vein is worked by a series of tunnels driven in on the vein, and now made 200 feet apart vertically . . . The fifth, or lowest tunnel, is now being driven in . . . the pay stratum in this shoot occupies the foot-wall portion of vein of quartz, which will average 8 feet in width. The size of the pay streak in this shoot is the same as it was in the fourth level above. The fifth level has still to be continued an additional length of 1,340 feet to cut under or through the paying ground opened and proved in the third and fourth levels . . . The paying portions of the vein, as in all the good quartz veins of this state, are represented by shoots of chimneys of productive quartz, with intervals of barren quartz between them. The Ariel ledge has five such shoots, beginning at the mouth of the tunnel and going west . . . The aggregate length on the vein, horizontally, of the productive ground, is therefore 810 feet.

These veins are opened, the water drained off, and the ores extracted entirely by tunnels. There are no draining or pumping shafts or machinery. As the ores come from the various levels, they are let down by an inclined track to the mills, which are situated directly below the fifth level . . . The main levels are 200 feet apart on the Ariel ledge. They have been opened far in advance of the requirements of the mills . . . Still deeper tunnels may be driven . . . to supply the mills for many years to come . . . The reserves (in the three ledges) are estimated at 111,944 tons with a gross value of $1,309,037 . . . Estimated cost of extracting and milling, $671,664.

From the (London) *Mining Journal* of August 1870, we have the following details of the first meeting of a Sierra Buttes Gold Mining Company and its purchase of the Sierra County Mine:

The directors congratulated the shareholders on the organization of the company, which was duly incorporated . . . on April 26, with a capital of 225,000 pounds in 112,500 shares of 2 pounds each . . . Since June 10 the mine has been worked on behalf of the company . . .[7]

That the new management brings new life to town and county is evident when we read in an earlier report (1871) statistics of June 1870, the month in which the mine began to operate under the London company:

> The total amount of quartz raised in the county during the year ending June 1, 1870, was 40,600 tons, which yielded $438,000. One hundred and ninety-three men were in the mines and mills throughout the year, and $135,244 was paid to them in wages. The following are the most prominent mines and their yield for the time indicated above: Alaska, $30,000; Gold Bluff, $37,222; Independence, $27,000; Sierra Buttes, $200,000; Brush Creek, $95,000.
>
> In this connection, an important change of proprietorship ought to be noticed, as showing the tendency of foreign capital to invest large amounts of money in mining property already developed and paying dividends . . . I refer to the sale of the celebrated Sierra Buttes Mine to an English company, which was concluded during the summer.[8]

After the mine's purchase, the new management lost no time in making a wagon road from the "City" up to the buildings at No. 7. A survey of the mine was made in 1871. The agent's report for that year describes many expensive improvements including additional boarding houses, store house, carpenter's and blacksmith's shops, three pans, one settler, and a turbine water-wheel to drive the same and more arrastras.[9]

After two years under the English company, Rossiter W. Raymond reports: "An aggregate of $550,000 in dividends has been paid to the English company, and further extensive improvements have been made, involving the expenditure of large sums of money."

In 1874, William Letts Oliver reports for the agent's three mills in operation; 9,608 tons were crushed by the Reis mill, 22,160 by the Hanks, and 21,768 by the Hitchcock. The ore contains .5 percent of sulphurets, which are amalgamated in pans after atmospheric condensation. The total bullion product was $479,608.41. Two hundred and fifty miners were employed at a wage of $50 per month and board. In the following year the number has been reduced to 240 and the wages are $2.50 to $3 per day, while foremen in the mine receive $5.42 per day.[10]

In a news item dated September 1876, we learn that "Mr. Frank Harland, for the past four years superintendent of the Sierra Buttes Mine, has resigned his position . . . Mr. William Johns, who for a long time has had supervision of Plumas Eureka and Sierra Buttes mines, is now at the Buttes."[11]

The Plumas Eureka Mine has been acquired by the Buttes Company and William Johns, the man for whom the town of Johnsville was named, is now the company's agent, replacing Messrs Cross & Co. but with the new title of general manager. Some months later, another mine, the Independence, "has fallen into the hands of the Sierra Buttes Co., and preparations are being made to pump out the water and take in quartz. To this end machinery is being made at the foundry in Downieville."[12]

With so much to occupy him, Mr. Johns may have lingered on until March 1878, when we learn of the arrival of E.M. Preston and I.B. Inch. There is also a new division of authority in the immediate management of the mine, Superintendent Preston, who comes directly from London, being responsible for all business details and direction of the surface working force, while Inch, soon to be replaced by William M. James, was to plan and supervise operations underground.

The striking of the "old blue-gravel channel," better known as the Big Blue Lead is reported in August 1870.[13] It must have cheered the new managers, for it was "rich in free gold." The early 80s were also years of prosperity for the mine, for when the eighth tunnel was begun in 1881, it too struck a ledge of "very rich quartz" and led to the erection of a new boarding house for the men.[14] The works were approaching Sierra City, and a mill at the town now seemed necessary.

In 1882, still another tunnel, No. 9, was started several hundred feet below No. 8, nearly level with the stage road, and by July 1883, the foundations of the new mill were being laid below the stage road and near the river. "Two hundred thousand dollars would probably be expended before any return could be realized from the lower levels of the mine. It was reported that the company has found it necessary to levy an assessment."[15]

But the *Sierra Tribune* (published in Sierra City) remained optimistic.

As this is the best paying mine, not only in Sierra County, but also one of the best in

California, it is entitled to more than passing mention from time to time . . . Tunnel No. 8 is now in over 3,000 feet. No. 9 tunnel was started three years ago. This tunnel is now in 3,700 feet. Eventually it will be run 9,000 feet. At 6,000 feet it is expected to strike the pay ledge, 700 feet below the present workings.

Last July work was begun on a 40-stamp mill at No. 9 tunnel, and this week 20 stamps commenced crushing ore from No. 8 tunnel. The ore is transported from that point to the mill on a double-track tramway 1,400 feet in length . . . The dimensions of the new mill are 98 by 85 feet and 81 feet high . . . The mill is supplied with eight Frue concentrators, Hendy's self feeders, and a Blake rock-breaker. Outside of this, the entire machinery has been furnished by Forbes & Taylor of the Downieville foundry.[16]

The cost, together with the added expense of the new chlorination works might well be a matter of concern to the company in London. Thanks to the invaluable *Mining and Scientific Press*, we are again present at a shareholders' London meeting[17] in April 1885, where President Tendron is speaking.

He tells the shareholders that while the tonnage stamped during the last half-year was 29,740 tons, a large increase over former periods for some time, the value of the gold and silver in that mineral was $6.12 as against $7.50. The falling off was due to a poorer quality of ore between the seventh and sixth levels. Still with increased tonnage and working costs reduced there was a profit. President Tendron's hopes for the new chlorination works were not too sanguine. In the following February, it was reported that "the output of the mine had increased several thousand dollars per month since the process of saving and working the sulphurets was introduced. Previously the tailings from the mills were sold to parties who worked the arrastras and realized large profits, the company thus sustaining a direct loss."[18]

Two years later, however, "the No. 9 tunnel is in a distance of 8,600 feet and still going ahead" but no vein had been found.[19] Worse still is the *Mountain Messenger's* news in October 1889: "The Buttes mine has closed down all below No. 3," and a November item is still worse: "Only 30 men employed at the Sierra Buttes Mine."[20]

From its beginning in 1850, we have carried the mine to nearly the end of its 39th year. Let us pause here to insert a survey of its work made in the mid-80s:

> The Sierra Buttes Mine, beginning . . . at the very incipiency of quartz mining in California, . . . has gone on expanding year by year, until it has reached its present large proportions and great perfections, having proved self-sustaining all the while. From the primitive arrastra, the next step was to the crude stamp mill, which . . . underwent steady improvement and enlargement, the final outcome being the incomparably complete Yuba mill now doing duty at the mouth of the main tunnel . . . As with the milling arm of the service, so with

the work of exploitation. It, too, was advanced by feeble stages, progressing from the open cut to the shaft; then came the short tunnel followed by others of greater length, no less than nine of these adits (entrances) having been driven, the last, longest and lowest of the series, being a very costly structure. Even the labor force have been promoted according to merit. Men who have shown themselves deserving have been advanced from subordinate to higher positions . . . this unfolding service having been closely adhered to . . . There has been worked out here a great success. The Sierra Buttes stands today, in so far as intelligent, persistent, and well directed effort is concerned, among the very best conducted quartz milling enterprises in the world . . .

During the last 14 years there has been taken from this mine the gross sum of $2 million, of which $1,360,288 has been disbursed to the shareholders in dividends; no assessments have ever been levied on the shares . . . The number of men employed in the mines and mills averages about 250. The Sierra Buttes ore . . . is of rather low grade, the average yield for the last 10 years being only about $7 per ton. It might, of course, have been assorted to a higher grade, some of the poorer quality being rejected. And this, had the mills been of limited capacity, might have been the very proper course to pursue. But it has been the policy of this company from the first to reduce anything that would afford any profit, however small, supplying milling facilities to that end. By this plan the life of the mine has been prolonged, while it has been made to yield up all that was in it. Great benefits would have accrued had this policy been more generally adopted by California mine owners, who have too often sacrificed the life of their properties for immediate results. This Sierra Buttes management has taught our people a lesson they would do well to heed. No commercial or manufacturing concern ever conducted its affairs more in conformity to strictly business principles than this company has done.[21]

Another tribute to the old mine (seemingly designed as its obituary) appears, dated Nov. 16, 1889, and with the heading, "A Worked-Out Mine," in the state's mining journal:[22]

The Sierra Buttes Mine, Sierra County, is called a worked-out mine because it is now turning out about $8,000 a month. It is among the oldest of California's quartz mines, having worked continuously for some 30 years or more. Prior to 1870, when it was acquired by the present company, it had produced $1,955,050. From 1870, to June this year: the value of the gold produced was $6,369,425, and dividends paid during the same period amounted altogether to $1,574,665, or $15.16 per share. The total production of gold from this mine has been $8,324,475.

This has been a pretty good record for any one mine. Of late its force has been reduced, for its ore at the lowest levels has been poor for a year or more. Several hundred men were formerly employed. The company, however, owns a fine producing mine in Plumas County, and lately purchased another producing one in Shasta County. The owners are English capitalists. There is a fine, 60-stamp mill belonging to the Sierra Buttes Mine, as well as an old mill up on the mountain side. The company also owns valuable water rights in Sierra County. The Sierra Buttes is the deepest gold mine in the world. Its lowest workings are 3,000 feet below the surface on a vertical line, and its lower, or No. 9 tunnel is about 9,000 feet in length. The ledge is still of good size and well defined at the face of the lowest tunnel, but is of low grade. It is possible, however, that a 'chimney' may be struck in some portion of the mine which will yet pay. But even if the mine is closed altogether, it has made a good record and a lot of money. The town of Sierra City was supported for some years mainly by this mine. Now the Young America, producing $30,000 a month, is looked upon as the mainstay of that section.

After 43 years of uninterrupted prosperity, who can tell what would have been the future of the great mine had not the forces of nature — the tragic fire of August 1889 followed by the destructive avalanches of January 1890 — to combine against it?

The Young America Mine

Even as the first and greatest of the mines on the mountain seemed to be in decline, Sierra City's hopes began to be fixed upon a new ledge that gave early promise of rivaling or even exceeding the record of Sierra Buttes. Various stories of the accident that led to its discovery long remained in circulation. The first account credited an anonymous sheepherder, who as he led his flock near the top of the ridge above the Sardine Lakes, chanced to pick up

The Young America Mine. *Thomas Family Photo*

a lump of quartz whose surface bristled with pieces of free gold. Distrusting his own judgment, he asked the opinion of the first wanderer he happened to meet. It was Oliver Sunderhaus, who, on examining the find, pronounced it worthless, "nothing but iron pyrites — fool's gold. The hills are full of rocks like this."

Carelessly, it was tossed aside, but one of the two marked well where it lay, and that one was not the hapless sheep-herder, of whom history gives no further accounts, other than to note he is no longer mentioned in any later version of the mine's discovery and that there were rumors of foul play.

What use will Sunderhaus, no miner, make of this clue to a fortune he carries in his pocket? We know that he was living near the lakes, employed in guarding the Sierra Buttes flumes, and was wise enough to make long and eager search of the vicinity for any signs of rocks resembling the speci-men he had taken from the sheepherder. One mile south of Packer Lake, he thought he had at last found the ledge, and straightway carried his tale and his gold-glittering quartz to certain friends of German extraction in Sierra City, through whom it speedily reached the ears of one of the town's most prominent citizens, none other than August Busch. He was interested to the extent of consulting his good friend Philip Deidesheimer, of Virginia City fame,[1] then in charge of the Colombo mine.

Of the very interesting early history of what became the Young America mine, we find a vivid account in the "Decision of Judge F.D. Soward," dated Nov. 16, 1885, in the case of Frankl vs. Deidesheimer.[2]

It begins with the location of two mining claims on Oct. 3, 1883, on which day Philip Deidesheimer and G.H. Oliver

Sunderhaus located the "American Quartz Lode" near Packer Lake at a point on the north side of the ridge called "the discovery shaft," where the ledge was then exposed. At the same time, Watt Hughes and August C.P. Busch located the "Germania Quartz Lodge," adjoining the American on the northwest. Two extensions were later made to these claims, the first on Nov. 28, 1883, when J. Sunderhaus (father of Oliver) located Willow Quartz Lode to the east of American; the second on June 21, 1884, when C.A. Heringlake located the Young American Quartz Lodge to the northwest of Germania.

These two extensions were made for the benefit of the original owners of the American and Germania locations and deeded over. The owners were Busch, Sunderhaus, Hughes, and Deidesheimer, but a damage suit brought against the last named made it desirable to withdraw his name from the partnership, so that, up to March 25, 1885, legal title vested in the three.

Between November 1883 and June 1884, much had happened. Four men employed in developing the vein had met with discouraging results. The ledge in the discovery shaft had petered out, being found in only one place and no prospect obtained there. It was Watt Hughes who discovered the actual vein, and it "looked good from the start," but — it was going in the wrong direction! What to do?

From Judge Soward's opinion in the Deidesheimer case:

> These locations were afterwards surveyed by . . . a U.S. deputy mineral surveyor and the lines somewhat changed; notices were then posted on each, complying with the new survey and giving

names of original locators as locators of new locations . . . American and Willow locations never
joined each other until Hendel made his survey in
December 1883, and moved the American location
bodily down to the Willow . . . Hendel acted under
Busch's direction to move the locations to cover
as much of the (Sardine) Lake side as they could,
because good prospects had been found there and
the ledge opened in two places. This accounts for
the moving of the American location nearly 300
feet toward the lake....

Prior to the date of incorporation, Busch
expended over $5,000 in developing the mine.
No one else contributed anything in money. Sunderhaus and Hughes worked in the mine, but this
did not count for their full share of expenses.
Deidesheimer contributed nothing. Busch paid
for everything that was paid for, transacted all the
business; in fact, had as complete control of the
mine as he would have had, had he been its sole
owner . . . The Young America Extension was not
discovered until June 1884. The Young American
Consolidated Mining Co. was incorporated July
24, 1885, with capital stock of $2.5 million, divided
into 500,000 shares distributed as follows:

A.C. Busch, 249,980 shares
John Sunderhaus, 125,000 shares
Watt Hughes, 125,000 shares
C.A. Heringlake, 10 shares
Philip Deidesheimer, 10 shares

On Oct. 16, 1885, the above five were elected directors and took action reserving 100,000 shares for working capital, leaving to owners:

Watt Hughes, 100,000 shares
John Sunderhaus, 99,990 shares
A.C. Busch, 99,990 shares
C.A. Heringlake, 10 shares
G.H.O. Sunderhaus, 10 shares
Philip Deidesheimer, 10 shares
Matilda Deidesheimer, 99,990 shares

The original owners of the American and the Germania locations were Busch, Sunderhaus, Hughes, and Deidesheimer, each of whom gets one-fourth of the stock (except that 99,990 shares of Sunderhaus' fourth are issued to his father, 10 shares of Busch's interest go to Heringlake to make him a director.) Busch stated that he himself was entitled to 200,000 shares, and had the 100,000 issued to the Deidesheimer family because he had promised them to Mrs. Deidesheimer.

No experienced gold hunter would be surprised to learn that some troubles had beset the partners between December 1883, at the discovery of the new vein by Watt Hughes, and the finding of the rich Young America Extension in June 1884.

"Not long since," as the *Mountain Messenger*, tells it in 1885, "a shaft was down some distance and the pay streak almost pinched out. One of the nearly worn-out and discouraged owners offered his one fifth interest (100,000 shares) for $500. A tunnel was started below the shaft and very soon resulted in discovery of pay ore . . . 100,000 shares were sold for working capital at 40 and 10 cents a share. (It is now over $1 a share and has already paid some dividends for shareholders!)"

By March 25 of the following year (1885), decision had been reached to erect a ten-stamp mill to crush the already great accumulation of quartz in the lower tunnel, and a still lower tunnel had been started. A wagon road from Sierra City to the mine was almost finished, and by June 1, a boarding house was being rushed to completion for the working force, which, from the four originally employed, had grown to a total of 108 men. It was expected that a tramway to bring ore to the mill would be ready in August. Oliver Sunderhaus, superintendent of the growing mine, was re-elected Aug. 1.

The mill began to crush the ore on Aug. 22, 1885, and now, but 14 months after discovery of the Young America Extension, not only was the new mine in full operation, but a great accumulation of rich quartz assured the owners of profits not only to defray all their expenditures, but large enough to endow each of them with a small fortune! With what wisdom will they pursue their development of what may become one of the state's great mines, greater perhaps than either the Buttes or the Idaho?

Again, we are indebted to our good friend, the *Mountain Messenger*, for the following description of a gold mine in full operation:

Tuesday morning, Sept. 1, Mr. C.A. Heringlake, of the firm of Busch & Heringlake Sierra City, courteously invited Mrs. Geo. Black, and your correspondent to enjoy a carriage ride with him to the Young America quartz mine, 8 miles above Sierra City — 5 miles to the junction of the Sierra Valley and Young America roads (5,100 feet) and thence 3 miles to the quartz mill, at an altitude of 5,600 feet, passing over the Sierra Buttes flume, altitude 5,500 feet, and what might be termed the "rocky road to Dublin." We reached the boarding house in good season for dinner, where one of the best tables is spread ever seen in the mountains. Mr. Philip Deidesheimer, the genial secretary of the company and acting superintendent during the temporary absence of Mr. Sunderhaus, greeted our party and showed us through the mill and mine.

The mill overlooks Lower Sardine Lake, whose waters are clear as crystal, mirroring the beautiful and romantic scenery. This and the adjacent lake will soon be stocked with fish. Ten stamps are now running, and that number will shortly be doubled. Four Frue concentrators will soon be used. Amalgam is removed from the silver plates each 24 hours, of the average ore worth, $125 a ton, 55 percent gold and 45 mercury. An assay office will soon be completed . . . The inner plates on both sides of the stamps were thickly coated with amalgam, as shown to us with a mirror. The Blake rock breaker used here can crush enough ore for a 40-stamp mill. An ore bin will be put in above the mill, with

capacity of 2,000 tons, so that in case storms stop
the running of the tramway, there will be sufficient
quartz stored to supply the mill for three months.
A track will be laid to the rock breakers for transportation of the ore. The brittle, fine quartz sent
down from the mill in sacks, averages $150 per ton.
The mill is in an air line from the highest peak of
the Sierra Buttes, about 2 to 3 miles. Six hundred
feet of flume carries water from the Upper Sardine
Lake, affording 180 feet of pressure. A new dam
will soon be constructed, above that of the Sierra
Buttes, to raise the water 6 to 8 feet.

Between here and Gold Lake are three lakes,
Packer and Upper and Lower Salmon, one almost
above another, in an irregular mass of rock and
debris; and around Gold Lake are many nameless
lakes. By trail to Gold Lake from the Sierra Buttes
flume the distance is about 7 miles. The cost of the
young America road was $1,000. The sulphurets
are worth $1,100 per ton. The length of the tram-
way is 3,300 feet, and cost $6,000. There are 64
buckets, each holding 100 pounds; and 160 tons
are brought down in 10 hours from the lower tunnel, 900 feet above the mill. The tramway speed
is 200 feet per minute, with break at each terminus . . . It is 1 mile from the mill by the trail to the
lower tunnel, and 1 mile to the upper . . . Snow
falls to the depth of 12 feet, but there is no danger of snow slides. A large building is being put up
above the boarding house for the company's office
and other purposes . . . 90 men are employed. In a

very limited time have these results been attained, and are most creditable to all concerned.

We started a foot up the trail from the mill to the mine, preceded by Mr. Deidesheimer, who rode on one of the tramway buckets . . . The altitude of the lower tunnel is 6,400, and that of the upper, 6,500. A telephone line is to connect the mill with mine and also with Sierra City. The shaft is 260 feet above the upper tunnel, and the altitude of the summit of the ridge is 7,100. The lower tunnel is in 600 feet, and air is furnished by a fan or blower . . . The upper tunnel is in about the same distance. In both tunnels icy cold water trickles down, and is caught in cans and barrels for drinking purposes. More ore is being taken out and milled. Water is soon to be brought to the mine and mill from the Young America Lake.[3]

The Young America location extends north of the Sierra Buttes . . . The pitch of the ledge is 40 degrees. All through the slopes the quartz is soft and brittle, sparkling with gold; and the ledge is in width 40 feet or more and must extend to an indefinite length down the mountain, and perhaps under Sardine Lakes to the ledges beyond. We noticed several patches of snow on the north side of the Sierra Buttes, one in a ravine 100 feet deep, part of which is said to have lain there over a quarter of a century. The snow is almost as hard as ice, melting mostly by evaporation and slowly at this high altitude — the head-center of the winter storms.

The officers of the Young America Mine are: A.C. Busch, president and treasurer; J.P. Deidesheimer, secretary; Philip Deidesheimer, agent; W.H. Mead, John Sunderhaus, Watt Hughes, A.C. Busch and A.C. Heringlake, trustees; G.H.O. Sunderhaus, superintendent; Wm. W. Casserly, foreman.

About 4 p.m., descending the steep, zigzag trail down the mountain to Upper Sardine Lake, Mr. Deidesheimer treated our party to a boat ride around this beautiful sheet of water, a mile long and one-half mile wide, 'neath the lofty snow-crowned Sierra Buttes, looming far above in the heavens, 8,950 feet above the sea, whose sentinel peaks have been and will forever be the guardian of the vaults of gold. (Signed d.)

We are grateful to what must have been an exhausted party for the only account of the mine which I have found giving the exact location not only of the buildings, but of the lode itself. We now see it to be distant from what Oliver Sunderhaus mistook for it when he began his shaft near Packer Lake. By an odd coincidence, the rich discovery is close to the Upper Sardine, "the beautiful little one with the unflattering name," which George and Bliss Hinkle, in their *Sierra Nevada Lakes*, describe as "fitting every requirement" of the lost Gold Lake as described by Greenwood and others.

We shall not again meet the agreeable young secretary, Philip Deidesheimer, Jr., who was soon to resign his position to become superintendent of a mine in Mexico. In June of this same year, Stephen Moore became superintendent of the Young America,[4] and in September the damage suit against the senior Deidesheimer is on trial in the State Supreme Court. Apparently no settlement was reached, for in April 1888, we learn that Frankl vs. Deidesheimer is to be tried in Plumas County. While one of the partners is thus occupied, A.C. Busch is resigning as supervisor, and Oliver Sunderhaus has gone to San Francisco to enjoy life in the big city, after taking a bond (option) on the Young America.[5] At the same time we are assured that Superintendent Moore "is doing ably."

A severe earthquake occurred April 28, 1888, in which "thousands of tons of rock were shaken from the Buttes," reminding us of the 1872 earthquake in Yosemite described by John Muir. It is not surprising that the Young America boarding house received some damage from this one.

In January 1889, the mine announced a cleanup of $27,200, dividends of $370,000, and the striking of a ledge 800 feet above the workings.[6] In July of the following year the news is still cheerful: "The famous Young America Mine is doing well. They have about 145 men on the payroll. They are pushing the No. 4 tunnel ahead, which will tap the ledge on a level with the ore house. There is plenty of good rock in sight for a number of years."[7] Officers elected at the end of August were: president and superintendent, Philip Deidesheimer; secretary, John C. Hughes; treasurer, John Sunderhaus; directors Watt Hughes, A.C. Busch, Thomas Brennan, Philip Deidesheimer, and John Sunderhaus.

On Aug. 29, Oliver Sunderhaus and wife were at the mine, but "thinking of taking a trip to Europe." But in the *Sierra Tribune*, published in Sierra City, of this same date, we are told that G.W. Hughes had been elected superintendent, succeeding Deidesheimer: "Mr. G. W. Hughes is no novice of the business of mining. For many years a resident of this banner county, for a long period he was actively engaged in that branch of industry. In the palmy days of the Keystone, Mr. Hughes was its superintendent . . . Mr. Hughes has a large fund of good, hard business sense, combined with strict integrity."[8]

What had happened since that late August election? We know only what we read one short week later under the heading, Young America Mine Changes: "Thomas Brennan and G.W. Hughes, superintendents; vice Deidesheimer; J.J.C. Hughes, secretary; Dr. Spedding mine physician; present management will pull together loose timbers which have been going adrift for past year. The mine needs only proper handling to get it into good condition . . . Present management are men of experience and integrity."

But a week later comes a not too cheerful note: "A.C. Busch inspected Young American Mine with new superintendent. Everything is to be done for benefit of stockholders. William Perryman is appointed foreman, vice, A. Leffler. One hundred-seventy men were employed up to last payment; 30 dismissed and more to follow." (Our informative *Sierra Tribune* discontinued publication at the end of 1890, a year of disasters for Sierra City.)

Nearly a year has passed before we hear again from Young America, and the implication is plain that what had happened to the Sierra Buttes Mine after 40 years of successful operation has befallen the Young America after a mere six: It has lost its vein, and entered into borrasca, but not without "firing another round of shots."

It is August 1891, and John Henderson, a mining engineer of long and varied experience in mines in the county, is the new superintendent. "A new ore body has been encountered in Tunnel No. 4 on the west end of the mine. The ore has not been yet tested, but the presence of copper is considered a good indication. The mine has produced $1,389,235 up to August of 1891, and has paid in dividends $490,000. This is our last word of the Young America Mine in operation.[9]

But alas! On Oct. 15, 1892, we read what may be the mine's obituary: "The Young America has lain idle for nearly two years. This was one of the bonanzas, but through recklessness and extravagant management (or mismanagement) its career has been varied and shorter lived than it should have been. Mr. A.C. Busch has now a controlling interest and it is his purpose to recommence operations this fall or the coming season. The mine was opened to the 2,200 foot level, connecting with a 3,000 foot tunnel. Much of the old works have caved and it is the intention now to work from the surface downward."[10]

Three years later: "The Young America quartz mine and mill with about 150,000 tons of tailings will be sold at auction next Tuesday. The property was bid in by W.P. Veuve and for $11, 339.48."[11] A trustee sale advertisement appeared in the April 4, 1896, and two subsequent issues of the Mining and Scientific Press. [12]

In May of 1896: "The Young America Mine in Sierra County was sold by John Bermingham, Jr., president of the California Powder Works, last Thursday to David P. Green of Chicago for $13,000. The new owner has considerable money and will reopen the mine this season."[13]

I seem to hear my Father replying to one expressing the theory, "Any fool could run a rich mine."

"Change that verb to *ruin* and I will agree with you."

Endnotes

Foreword

1. A.K. Hamilton Jenkin, *The Cornish Miner*, (London: Allen & Unwin, 2nd edition, 1948) 321-331.

2. Cornwall and West Devon Mining Landscape is a UNESCO and World Heritage Site. Designated in 2006, the area is celebrated as "testimony to the contribution Cornwall and West Devon made to the Industrial Revolution in the rest of Britain and to the fundamental influence the area had on the mining world at large". http://whc.unesco.org/en/list/1215

Introduction: The Cornish Capital of America

1. A.K. Hamilton Jenkin, *The Cornish Miner*, 321-331

2. F.E. Halliday, *A History of Cornwall*, (London: Gerald Duckworth & Co., 1959) 298.

Chapter 1: We Go Above

1. The New York House, later Deer Creek Inn

2. A year later, time of departure was advanced to 6 a.m., due to, according to the *Mountain Messenger* (Sept. 25, 1886), refusal of the postmaster to deliver mail at an earlier hour.

3. *Historic Spots of California*, by Mildred Brooke Hoover and H.E. and E.G. Rensch, revised by Ruth Teiser (Stanford University Press, c1948) 121.

4. J.L. Wolfe, *Yuba River Canyon Country Bulletin*, No. 56, (Grass Valley, CA: Grass Valley Chamber of Commerce, 1932-33) Nos.1-56, mimeographed. See also Ibid., No. 11.

[5] Historic Spots of California, 125.

[6] J.L. Wolfe, *Yuba River Canyon*, No. 56.

[7] Doris Foley, "English Dam catastrophe hastened Sawyer decision," *Nevada City Nugget: 100 years of Nevada County, 1851-1951*, 50-52; also Doris Foley and S. Griswold Morley, "The 1883 Flood on the Middle Yuba River, *California Historical Society Quarterly*, v.28, No. 3, Sept. 1949, 233-242.

[8] J.L. Wolfe, *Yuba River Canyon*, No. 56

[9] Ibid., No. 12. See also *Historic Spots in California*, 1948, 207-208.

[10] Edmund Kinyon, *The Northern Mines* (Grass Valley-Nevada City Union Pub. Co., 1949) 106.

[11] Alexandre Dumas, *The Journal of Madame Giovanni*, translated from the French edition (1856) by Marguerite E. Wilbur (New York: Liveright, 1944) 195-196.

[12] *Nevada City Nugget 100 years*, p.49; also *Oakland Tribune*, Knave section, Oct. 7 to 28, 1945.

[13] Many complaints in Nevada City papers roused the *Downieville Messenger* to remark that it is not the duty of the Sierra County sheriff to hunt our robbers around Nigger Tent, but he will make arrests if warrants are sworn out. See Edmund Kinyon, *Northern Mines*, 108-111.

[14] Edmund Kinyon, *Northern Mines*, 108

[15] *California: A Guide to the Golden State*, Federal Writers' Project (New York: Hastings House, 1939).

[16] Alexandre Dumas, *Madame Giovanni*, 201-202.

[17] J.L. Wolfe, *Yuba River Canyon*, No. 56.

Chapter 2: The Old Man Watches the Sky

[1] "Sierra City...was first settled in 1850 by gold miners. The vicinity was full of Indian rancherias or camp sites and apparently was one of the most heavily populated Indian districts in

California." *Calif. Division of Mines, Geologic Guidebook along Highway 49,* Sept. 1948, 84.

2 Robert Welles Ritchie, *The Hell-roarin' Forty-niners* (New York: J.H. Sears Inc., 1928)144.

3 Illustrated History of Plumas, Lassen & Sierra Counties (San Francisco: Fariss & Smith, 1882) 870.

4 "Manuel Gutierrez, an old prospector at Sierra Buttes and discoverer of the Reis (or Sierra Buttes) Mine and of the Hawkeye, Independence, and Eureka, has recently opened a very rich mine." *Mining and Scientific Press,* San Francisco, CA, 22:340, June 17, 1871.

5 "In August, 1869, a piece of gold, weighing 95½ pounds, was taken from the Monumental Mine in this county. Its original weight, indeed is said to have been 140 pounds, but a piece is said to have 'become detached'. Some $70,000 has been extracted from the mine during the short time it has been in operation.

"We take pleasure in giving the following particulars in regard to the great California nugget: This, the largest piece of gold ever found in California, was taken out of the Monumental quartz mine, situated about 12 miles north of Downieville, at the Sierra Buttes. It weighs 1,142.25 ounces, or 95½ pounds, as cleaned, and is almost pure gold, being valued at $21,156.52.

"The Monumental quartz mine is owned by Messrs. Wm. A. Farrish & Co., and located upon the same mountain as the Sierra Buttes and Independence mines … Work was begun on the mine about the 1st of July by sinking upon the vein a narrow ledge, varying from 12 to 48 inches, and filled with decomposed quartz. It paid from the surface. The nugget was found at a depth of 25 feet from the top, on the 18th of August, A.T. Farrish & Co." See also Henry G. Hanks, *Second Annual Report of the State Mineralogist, 1882,* "Famous Gold Nuggets," 147-150.

6 *Illustrated History,* Fariss & Smith, 1882, 471.

Chapter 3: Boom-town of the Eighties

[1] George and Bliss Hinkle, *Sierra Nevada Lakes* (Indianapolis: Bobbs-Merrill Co., 1949) 107, 214.

[2] *The Sierra County Tribune* remained in Sierra City until it ceased publication in December 1890.

[3] *Sierra Tribune,* Nov. 21, 1890.

[4] Ibid., Nov. 9, 1888.

[5] *Overland Monthly,* Volume II, Second Series, "Up in the Sierras" (San Francisco: Samuel Carson, publisher, July 1883) 44-48.

[6] "Springs and waterfalls emerging from glacio-fluvial deposits along Sardine Creek, Sierra County... The falls are close beside Highway 49." *Geologic Guide along Highway 49, Sierran Gold Belt: The Mother Lode Country* (Calif. Division of Mines and Geology, Bulletin 141, 1948).

[7] A logging camp let on contract for felling timber for the mine. *Sierra Tribune,* June 6, 1888.

[8] Named after the Reis brothers, former owners of the Sierra Buttes Mine. After 1870, when the mine was sold to the Sierra Buttes Mining Co., the ravine began to be more commonly known as Buttes Ravine.

[9] A pioneer settler in Sierra City who had earlier been one of the first prospectors along the North Fork.

[10] *Mountain Messenger,* Dec. 29, 1884.

Chapter 4: Up the Trail

[1] "The Comstock Lode may truthfully be said to be the tomb of the forests of the Sierras. Millions on millions of feet of timber are annually buried in the mines never more to be resurrected... Not less than 80 million feet of timber and lumber are annually consumed on the Comstock Lode. In a single mine, the Consolidated Virginia, timber is being buried at the rate of 6 million feet per annum, and in all other mines in like

proportion. At the same time about 250,000 cords of wood are consumed. The pine forests of the Sierra Nevada Mountains are being drawn upon for everything in the shape of wood or lumber, and have been thus drawn upon for many years." Dan DeQuille (William Wright), *History of the Big Bonanza*, (Reprint of the 1876 edition, New York: Knopf, 1947) 174.

2 Beginning at the place of the mine's discovery in 1850, the first and uppermost tunnel pierced the mountain-side at about the 7,000-foot level. As the vein proceeded downward, this tunnel became known as No. 1, successive numbers being used to indicate the various other levels. In the 1880s, No. 9 was driven just under the stage road in Sierra City and in Buttes Ravine, a short distance above the river.

3 *Pinus lambertiana.* These royal pines grow 200 to 300 feet tall, and live from 500 to 800 years, growing 10 or even 12 feet thick. The great cones, the largest pine cones, 16 to 25 inches long and 16 inches in diameter ... are borne pendant on the tips of the wide spreading branches. Elinor Shane Smith, *Trees of the Yosemite and of the Sierra Nevada*, c. 1929.

4 Louise M Roope Griswold, A *Woman's Pilgrimage to the Holy Land* (Hartford, Conn.: J.B. Burr and Hyde, 1871.)

5 *Messenger* Feb. 27, 1886.

6 Ibid., March 28, 1885, "J. Rawlings of Sierra City replies to several slanderous articles by T.P. Williams."

7 Ibid., Oct. 2, 1886.

Chapter 5: Snowshoes and Sleigh Bells

1 *Messenger,* Jan. 23, 1886.

2 Ibid., Jan. 12, 1889. "Horses' snowshoes are made of thin plates, about 9-by-11 inches, fastened to hoofs with clamps. Horses are shod with long heel calks, which go through snow shoe and prevent slipping when going up and down hill. A horse can travel four or five miles an hour on shoes."
The trip from Sierra City to Nevada City was made by horses

on shoes in two days, weather permitting, an overnight stop being made at Camptonville.

[3] Ibid., Feb. 25, 1882.

[4] "Dope was apt to be made out of anything, including hemlock and pine tar, turpentine, cedar oil, glycerin, tallow, camphor, and castor oil ... Skiing was first introduced into California about 100 years ago by Scandinavian miners at the Gold Rush camps of the 1850s, Johnsville, La Porte, Poker Flat, Howland Flat, Downieville and others." Jerry Carpenter, *California Winter Sports and the Eighth Winter Olympic Games*, Fearon Publishers, as quoted in the *Oakland Tribune*, March 9, 1958.

Chapter 6: Summertime on the Mountain

[1] Names derived from reading Albion Tourgee's *A Fool's Errand*, a novel of reconstruction in the South, in which the heroine is a notable horsewoman.

[2] The resemblance of this lake to the lost "Gold Lake," described by Stoddard and others in 1849 and 1850 is pointed out by George and Bliss Hinkle in *Sierra Nevada Lakes*, (Indianapolis: Bobbs-Merrill Co., 1949) 107-8.

[3] "Cups," we always called it, but the name appeared on one old map as "Cuffs." The meadow itself disappeared, having been invaded by an advancing forest of Douglas Firs.

[4] Brother George was one of our group of licensed local preachers, who would seem to have been imported from the old country, in accordance with a saying of John Wesley, the father of Methodism: "Give me 100 preachers who fear nothing but sin and desire nothing but God, and I care not a straw whether they be clergymen or laymen, such alone will shake the gates of hell."

[5] The name given to a meadow near the river, acquired by the Sierra Buttes Co. as a site for its new office and several other buildings, one of them the new chlorination works.

[6] *Prunus subcordata.* "Other names: Western wild, Klamath, Hog or Pacific Plum ... Range: From central Oregon (east

of the Coast Ranges) and southward through northeastern California and the northern Sacramento Valley to the Yosemite Valley (up to 4,000 feet) and south in the inner Northern Coast ranges to Lake County … Wild plums make more fragrant and delicious preserves than cultivated ones, as every good housewife knows, and this one cooks to a confection not inferior to the wild plum jams of the eastern states. Around Grass Valley and Sierra City and elsewhere in the Mother Lode country, you can often pick up a few jars set out for sale to the summer tourist and, whatever they cost, they will be worth it." Donald Culross Peattie, *A Natural History of Western Trees* (Boston: Houghton Mifflin Co., 1953).

7 J.L. Wolfe, *Yuba River Canyon*, No 36.

Chapter 7: The Queen's Jubilee Caps a Year of Novelty

1 *Messenger*, March 1, 1884.

2 Ibid., Dec. 8, 1886.

3 Ibid., June 25, 1887.

Chapter 8: Our Mountain Town is Quarantined

1 The Hitchcock, a very large mill at No. 7, had been crushing ore left on dump by first owners of the mine. It was replaced by a cheaper structure on the site of the old Hanks Mill. *Mountain Messenger*, Oct. 8 and Nov. 12, 1887.

2 Ibid., June 25, 1887.

3 Ibid., Aug. 1887.

4 *Sierra Tribune*, Feb. 17, 1888.

5 *Messenger*, Feb. 11, 1888.

6 Ibid., April 7, 1888.

7 *Sierra Tribune*, April 20 and May 18, 1888.

8 Ibid., April 27 and May 11, 1888.

9 Ibid., June 2, 1888.

Chapter 9: Our Patriotic Holidays

[1] *Messenger*, July 11, 1888.

[2] Ibid., July 7, 1888.

Chapter 10: Our Alpine Winter

[1] *Messenger*, Oct. 9, 1889.

[2] Ibid., Nov. 2, 1889.

[3] *Messenger*, Jan. 11, 1890.

[4] Buttes Saddle Mine is situated under the crest of the Sierra Buttes at an elevation of nearly 7,000 feet. – California State Mining Bureau, *Report of State Mineralogist* for two years ending Sept. 15, 1892.

[5] Sierra County Tribune, Jan. 31, 1890.

[6] Ibid., Feb. 14, 1890.

[7] Ibid., Feb. 7, 1890.

[8] *Mountain Messenger*, Feb. 22, 1890.

Chapter 11: Jack Tremain Comes Home

[1] Cornish cream, often called Devonshire or clotted, is a great table delicacy, consisting of the fresh cream that clots on the top of new milk when it is heated very slowly in a wide, shallow pan." Dorothy Gladys Spicer, *An English Oven* (New York: Women's Press, 1948).

Afterword

[1] "Why We Lead the World," San Francisco *Examiner*, June 8, 1893, page 3.

[2] "Librarian Asks Not So Much of Questions Asked as of their Use," *Oakland Tribune*, Aug. 5, 1929, page 2

[3] *California Librarian*, July 1965, page 183.

Appendix 1: Sutter Buttes Mine

[1] *Mining and Scientific Press*, 13:290, Nov. 10, 1866.

2 Bothwick, J.D., *Three Years in California* (Edinburgh and London, 1857).

3 *The Bay of San Francisco, a History* (Chicago, Lewis Pub. Co., 1892) 1:427-9

4 Christian had a distinguished career in San Francisco, being "three times the City Treasurer (in 1882, 1886, and 1888). He was prominent in the Society of California Pioneers, of which he was president in 1894." Ibid.

5 *Mining and Scientific Press*, 20:428, June 25, 1870.

6 Henry Janin, "Report on the Sierra Buttes Mine" (In Rossiter W. Raymond, *Statistics of Mines and Mining in the States and Territories West of the Rocky Mountains* (Washington, D.C., Government Printing Office, 1870) 60-61.

7 *Mining Journal* London, 40: 697, Aug. 20, 1870.

8 Raymond, *3rd Annual Report*, 1871.

9 Ibid., *4th Annual Report*, 1873, 138-40.

10 Ibid., *7th Annual Report*, 1875, and *8th Annual Report*, 1877.

11 *Mining and Scientific Press*, 33:205, Sept. 23, 1876.

12 Ibid., 34:229, April 14, 1877.

13 Rodman W. Paul, *California Gold* (Harvard University Press, 1947) 100-105. "The largest dead river is known as the "Big Blue Lead," and has been traced from Little Grizzly in Sierra County, to Forest Hill in Placer County, a distance of 65 miles." — Rossiter W. Raymond, *Statistics of Mines and Mining in the States and Territories West of the Rocky Mountains* (Washington, D.C., Government Printing Office, 1879). Quoted from John S. Hittell in *Overland Monthly*.

14 *Mining and Scientific Press*, 42:209, April 2, 1881.

15 Ibid., 47:37, July 21, 1883.

16 Ibid., 48:238, April 5, 1884. (Reprinted from the *Sierra Tribune*.)

17 Ibid., 50:314, May 16, 1885.

[18] Ibid., 52:148, Feb. 27, 1886.

[19] Ibid., 56:252, April 21, 1888.

[20] Ibid., 59:358, Nov. 9, 1889.

[21] *Gold Mines and Mining in California* (S.F. George Spaulding & Co., 1885) 288-293.

[22] *Mining and Scientific Press*, 59:380, Nov. 16, 1889.

Appendix 2: The Young America Mine

[1] In 1861, Philip Deidesheimer invented the method of "timbering in square sets," first used in mines on the Comstock Lode, where he was superintendent of the Ophir Mine.

[2] Opinion on merit, Frankl vs. Deidesheimer, Sierra County Superior Court, L.B. Frankl, plaintiff, Philip Deidesheimer, et. al., Defendants. *Mountain Messenger*, Nov. 21, 1885.

[3] Young America Lake is the higher of two lakes between Upper Sardine Lake and the summit of the Sierra Buttes.

[4] *Mountain Messenger*, June 19, 1886.

[5] Ibid., Feb. 3 and 25, 1888.

[6] *Mining and Scientific Press*, 58: 118, Feb. 16, 1889.

[7] Ibid., 61: 68, Aug. 2, 1890.

[8] Ibid., 61: 164, Sept. 6, 1890.

[9] Ibid., 63:146, Sept. 5, 1891.

[10] Ibid., 65:253, Oct. 15, 1892.

[11] Ibid., 71: 355, Nov. 30, 1895.

[12] Ibid., 72: 278, April 4,1896.

[13] Ibid., 72:355, May 2, 1896.

Acknowledgements

This story of my Aunt Mabel's girlhood in Sierra City has been with me for a very long time. Typed from her hand-written pages by my mother, Liliana Thomas, in the early 1960s, several copies were loaded into black imitation leather spring binders and ended up in the homes of Mabel's nieces and nephew. Nobody seems to remember what she intended to do with it and, strangely, she left no instructions.

In the decades since, as I raised my family and worked as a newspaper reporter and editor, I have tossed around in my mind the relevance of Mabel's story. Those years marked a declining interest in tales of gold mining and the Old West, replaced by interest in the overlooked historical role of different ethnicities in the state's development.

In 2010, on a camping trip to Sardine Lakes above Sierra City, I had a chance to walk through the old mine office, now owned by the Evan Daily family. Seeing the well-preserved rooms with historical photos of Sierra City's mining past on the walls woke me up. I saw how the town's past was being preserved by someone who loved it and how that was probably all that mattered. Aunt Mabel's story fit here and thus in the world in general. I knew it was time to get it done.

I had the immediate encouragement of my husband, Don Lattin, a great writer of people's stories. My dear friend

Ginny McPartland was my editor and advisor and constant cheerleader. Without her assistance, I would still be fretting and fuming over the whole thing.

Malcolm Margolin's Heyday Press was my beacon and inspiration with the way it has championed our state's complex human history through the fantastic books it has published. While Heyday unfortunately saw no place for it in the declining market for western Americana in 2015, Malcolm's praise for Aunt Mabel's manuscript and his insistence that I get it published anyway was deeply gratifying.

In contrast to those reports of declining interest, I have been buoyed by the enthusiastic reaction I have received from countless people about this project. Memoirs have become popular and that trend shows a well-observed and honestly written story from any era still has great appeal.

My heart-felt thanks to Mary Nourse, president of the Sierra County Historical Society, and Dianne Bruns, director of the Kentucky Mine Museum in Sierra City, who were excited by the prospect of this memoir and supplied me with facts and many of the photos reproduced throughout the book. In many ways, the publication of this memoir acknowledges and honors the 3,000 residents of one of the tiniest and least spoiled counties in California, a place that has survived the ravages of its gold mining past and now offers a wealth of natural beauty.

Another dear friend, photographer Celeste Greco, helped me restore and scan a dozen or more old family photos that survived in drawers without proper care for decades.

My friends Michael Bass and Carole Brown, both graphic artists of wild imagination, designed the cover and Margaret Copeland, the veteran of many book designs, helped me feel this strange print-on-demand project was within my capabilities. The three of them gave this book its lovely, refined and truly historical feel. I am very grateful.

I wish to acknowledge my older cousins, Richard, Stephen and Pam, who drew on many personal memories to help me recall things accurately. I wish my father Willard (Bill) Thomas were still here because he would be proud of this project as would my Aunts Ruth, Winifred and Marjorie. They all expected it of me anyway.

To my daughters Brigid and Allegra, who was born with the same head of black Cornish hair as Aunt Mabel's, I am grateful for their love and patience in listening to me. And I hope Aunt Mabel and my grandfather, whom we called Papu — my guiding spirits — are happy as well.

CPSIA information can be obtained
at www.ICGtesting.com
Printed in the USA
FSOW04n1138220717
36430FS

9 780692 818084